LOST FRAGMENTS
OF
PLAUSIBLE UNIMPORTANCE

LOST
FRAGMENTS
OF
PLAUSIBLE
UNIMPORTANCE

*Pointless Guidelines
for the Hopeless*

Michael Richard Lucas

SUNSTONE
PRESS

SANTA FE

Sunstone books may be purchased for educational, business, or sales promotional use. For information please write: Special Markets Department, Sunstone Press, P.O. Box 2321, Santa Fe, New Mexico 87504-2321.

Book and cover design › Vicki Ahl
Body typeface › ITC Benguiat Std
Printed on acid-free paper
∞
eBook 978-1-61139-564-8

Library of Congress Cataloging-in-Publication Data

Names: Lucas, Michael Richard, 1986- author.
Title: Lost fragments of plausible unimportance : pointless guidelines for the hopeless / by Michael Richard Lucas.
Description: Santa Fe : Sunstone Press, (2018)
Identifiers: LCCN 2018032245 (print) | LCCN 2018044088 (ebook) | ISBN 9781611395648 | ISBN 9781632932402 (softcover : alk. paper)
Subjects: LCSH: Ambivalence. | Despair. | Anecdotes. | Philosophy.
Classification: LCC BF575.A45 (ebook) | LCC BF575.A45 .L83 2018 (print) | DDC 128–dc23
LC record available at https://lccn.loc.gov/2018032245

WWW.SUNSTONEPRESS.COM
SUNSTONE PRESS / POST OFFICE BOX 2321 / SANTA FE, NM 87504-2321 /USA
(505) 988-4418 / ORDERS ONLY (800) 243-5644 / FAX (505) 988-1025

INTRODUCTION

I, MICHAEL R. LUCAS, discovered these writings at the university library while researching extinct flightless birds. They literally fell onto my lap. They were haphazardly shoved into another more prestigious book I happened to be studying at the time. Imagine my surprise when I began reading this bizarre, wonderful ramble. I've edited bits and pieces, yet, for the most part, the work remains here in its entirety, untouched.

As I have undertaken a great deal of background research on the text, I can conclude with an air of certainty that these fragments are the writings of a destitute member of the lower class who suffered from various neuroses or psychoses, or

a graduate scholar of perhaps theoretical physics or philosophy,

or an elaborate hoax carried out by a very witty humorist.

I'm not entirely certain. Your guess is as good as mine.

THE LOST FRAGMENTS

We are nothing. When we die nothing happens. When we are born nothing happens. When we do anything nothing happens. There is no center. We are jostling puzzle pieces perpetually molded by the surrounding universe. We are a collection of perspectives provided by other people. We attempt to embody these perspectives in order to exist and make sense of ourselves. We cling to a linear narrative through others, through ritual, through technology. We cling to a language of distraction that makes palatable our eternal demise. All we ever do, in every set of principles we put forth, in every scientific formula, in every to-do list is conjure up sedatives to make the thought of eternally floating across the galaxy in a million little pieces—seem like not a big deal. Perhaps some of us are better able to distract ourselves than others. I don't think this is a reason to celebrate.

My laundry was aimlessly spinning in the dryer. I watched it. Aimlessly. These were the thoughts that occupied my mind. I was sitting at the laundromat down the street from my apartment. Aimlessly built. This dependable wave of paranoid depression. Another way to keep me distracted and poor. I could let everything go. More so now than ever. I could walk out. Did my clothes need to be clean? Would I delay the inevitable demise of the universe if my clothes were dirty? That's a thought. The existence of everything depended entirely on the cleanliness of my clothes and my continued cooperation to wear them. Nothing told me it couldn't be so. By some strange cataclysmic sequence of cause and effect, leaving without my clothes would be the straw that broke the universal camel's back. In the end, it wasn't that I didn't want to witness the complete annihilation of existence itself. I just needed clean underwear for tomorrow.

I was walking down the street. I passed a man holding a sign. In large red letters it read "Repent!" He asked me if I was a god fearing man. I told him I was afraid of everything.

I had nothing. What I had prevented me from getting what I wanted. I had just enough to be pissed I didn't have more. I was good enough to be pissed I wasn't the best. What would the best even look like? What if I could have everything I ever wanted? Would I be able to want it if I had it? What would I change about my life if I could actually change it? Will it fit? I tried to fit all the clothes into one dryer, but the door deliberately swung open during the only moment it should have closed. So I had to start another load. All the times I thought I arrived on the peripheries of perfection. A small fish in a vast ocean of mediocrity. Once again. Everything that happened. It only built false confidence. But it never ends. Never. There is always something else. Always one more step. Always one more requirement to check off. Always one more pointless task to complete. I was stuck in purgatory. Forever rolling a boulder up a hill. Repeat. Repeat. When did this begin? This vicious cycle of mediocrity. That was the real problem. If I could pin down the starting dates, I could verify my eternal demise. My purgatorial residency. I could not discern when this had begun. I always felt like this. My childhood was an exception. I don't remember exactly. Perhaps this is the way life is? There was no way to tell. I vaguely remember saying that yesterday. And the day before.

The writer should infect the reader with their disease. And simultaneously supply the cure.

A box of condoms glided forward astride bananas flanked by a gallon of milk and a case of beer. The cashier and I stood. Silent spectators to this ceremonial procession. I reflected on my existence. This is the most and least responsible I will ever be in my life. I spent the later part of my twenties overworked, underpaid, stressed, drunk, and pissed off. That's not entirely true. But for the most part, yes. I was no longer in my twenties. I was no longer in that grocery store. Yet the same ridiculous store mascot (a genetically engineered smiley-face monkey-puppy) was winking at me. Attempting comfort. Attempting to communicate. It told me that wherever I went, this abomination was profiting off of my most basic needs and meticulously tracking my purchases. I hope my data-center guardian angels were proud to see their baby boy growing up before their security camera eyes. The beer had changed to wine. It's not much. But others made a religion out of less. I wouldn't prevent them from making me their Messiah. As long as I saw some of the benefits in this lifetime. For starters, *I* would replace the smiley-faced monkey-puppy as the new beacon of comfort and hope for the masses. I think I'd be good at it.

Just barely keeping it together. Impossible to express the terror and the fear brought on by the panic. The total loss of control. The lack of a remedy. In this world. No experts. No cure. In the universe. In the heavens. In other dimensions. In all eternity. Being lost to everything that could do anything. The only solution to end it all. It might also be a trick. But at least it might prevent you from hurting others. And it might provide the silence. It might not. You would also hurt others by ending it. In other ways. Can you hold on? This is the gamble. How do you know? There might be a reason to play the game. I do not know what it is.

I know that I am not *not* thinking.

Don't listen to anyone. You are always right. Trust your gut. Go with your first instinct. No matter what, you will make it. You will always find a way. Never give up. Never give up. I was writing this advice to someone on how to be successful. Wait, maybe not. Perhaps this was a warning about the mindset of a psychopath. I forgot to label it. It could be either, I'm not sure. Follow the above at your own discretion.

Everyone loves a good love story. This is not a good love story. I was trapped in a relationship that onlookers would confuse as a romantic endeavor. I was either falling deeper in love or I was planning on never speaking to her again. Every time I saw her. As soon as I was able to make up my mind, I became too exhausted to actually follow through with anything. Therefore, the world defaulted back to mundane sameness despite the tempest raging between my ears. Most of life was like this. I was not in love with her. I had been in love before. This was not love. She was not my lover. She was someone else's future lover. But right now she was the only person who appeared to enjoy me. She wasn't the worst person in the world. I told myself I could probably like her enough. I've been wrong about everything in my life. I've also been right about everything. And before I knew it, once again, I simply didn't care if we were together, we simply were, because nothing else happened. Nothing ever happens.

If I wrote a book about myself, I'm afraid I'd trap myself in-between the pages for all eternity. If I could create myself outside myself, this story would not do. Or would I be creating a whole other conscious Being by writing in this voice on these pages? Was I trapping this Being-voice within these pages? I certainly hope not. Perhaps a higher-lifeform had already trapped me within this much more advanced story-telling device of being human. All I am. A more advanced literary device. Than a book. A self-writing literature for a higher-lifeform. I keep my subservient voice-Beings within these pages and within my own head. I export them within the heads of others. I call it literature for entertainment purposes. The higher-lifeforms watch me act out my silly self-narrated antics from afar. This is their literature. Their version is more advanced. None-the-less. Our literature is cruel.

There is time for this. There will be time for that. There will always be time. I found myself spending an inordinate amount of time staring aimlessly out of windows. Especially for someone my age. I no longer cared if anyone caught me. Although from time to time I felt phony. It was fleeting. My thoughts often bitter discussions. People who have long exited my plane of existence. If they ever shared it. It's probably not a good sign. Someone this forgotten to be young. Was I still young? I have started thinking about my life in past tense. What is the prime of my life. When everything is supposed to be happening. I've always felt old. I've always been in the wrong place. I've always been in the wrong time. Any more or less then anyone else? Maybe. I've just been more aware. Slightly.

Guilt and shame are never felt by those who need to feel them. Only by those who feel them too much. Causing them to commit acts. Causing them to feel guilt and shame.

These days, we are constantly at war. Or on the brink of escalation. Escalation that will lead to all-out-war. Or we are just at war. Constantly. It's impossible to keep up. But perhaps all the information we receive about war (or nearly being at war) is another illusion to pacify the masses. To keep us anxiously at war with ourselves. Then again, I haven't been outside today. So the great war could be occurring right now. If the war were real, it could still be an illusion. It would probably be a better illusion if the war were real. Regardless of the outcome and various motives of this war, it hardly seems worth mentioning here. It has become increasingly difficult to determine if I have gone insane, or if the rest of humanity has gone insane. Perhaps we have all lost it together. If we ever had it to begin with. Humanity is an experiment conducted by a mad scientist without a control variable.

I was reading a popular magazine at the doctor's office. A recent survey found a surprising number of people thought "Ruthless dictators are kinda cute." The most common response provided: "I like a person who is dedicated to something—it doesn't matter what."

I remember a lovely Friday night. It comes back to me. Clearly now. After a long day at work. In the summer. I was all set to kill myself. Then I realized. When we die, what if we are merely subjected to silent witnesses of our previous lives for eternity? My only activity: sitting and watching everything up until this point. Everything up to this point had been shitty. Especially lately. I did not want to be stuck. Sitting. Watching. So instead, I continued drinking myself to the edge of oblivion. I woke up the next morning. My first thought. I should have killed myself.

I've always been in the wrong place at the wrong time because this isn't my life. Of all the bizarre possibilities that the multiverse has to offer, the strangest wouldn't be that someone else is playing the game of us. Our bodies would be the host to a form of remote-controlled game that higher-lifeforms can choose to play for entertainment purposes. Perhaps in their homes or at an arcade. They would have the actual controls to the game, and we would be stuck with the primordial illusory sense of cause and effect. This sense would justify all the smaller actions we control around us. Like choosing what we have for dinner. Like choosing what sitcoms we watch. This wouldn't be a very good reflection on the decision making skills for most of us. In case we got wise to the fact that we were merely being played as a game (a paranoid lunatic randomly made a lucky guess), we would find many other diluted versions of this same scenario dispersed among our popular narratives. It would even be found in serious philosophies. It would need to appear that this scenario had already been considered by the best, brightest, and most imaginative minds. How would you begin to imagine your way out of a predicament where everything would serve as a distraction? You would have no way to determine distraction from strategy. Every strategy would only serve to further distract. This should be distressing not because of how elaborate it sounds. It should be distressing because of its simplicity. With minor tweaks here and there, it already mirrors the way in which we operate on a daily basis. No problems ever get resolved in the world. Nothing ever really changes. However. Think of all the time and energy spent on making it appear as if radical change is happening around us all the time. But there are never any real answers. There are never any real questions. There never can be here. This is only a simulation. Here I was again. Staring. Another window. My humble apartment. It was raining outside. At least the mood fit.

From what I've gathered, conversing with god is similar to our high school attempts to converse with a popular teenager we wanted to date or be-friend. It would unfold as follows: we'd ask, "What do you want from me?" God would tease us, "Oh I dunno...a lot of impossible things." We would then ask, "What do you mean? Why is your message so confusing?" God responds with a charming smile, "Hmmmmmmmm, you'll find out. Eventually..." We ask, "When?" God answers coyly, "Um...sometime? Later?"

Yesterday, I returned to the couch to continue staring at the television. I felt an obligation to be pacified. In taking up this pursuit, I signed on to see it through to the end. Sure, when spelled out like this, my actions appear uselessly loyal. In my defense, we typically don't have to spell out the ridiculous actions we perform throughout our day. The action didn't seem as strange when it was buffered by the other subservient habits strongly encouraged by the absurd power hierarchies I compulsively placed myself under to keep me in check throughout the day. The show was a behind-the-scenes-look at the day-to-day life of a particularly popular actress. It was very boring. I was wildly disappointed.

I must have fallen asleep within a few minutes. Various commercials blended together in a dream. "Moments like these, the moments of your life." A commercial for laundry detergent had turned into a saccharin night-mare. The universe was sparkling clean. Everyone wore freshly pressed pastel yachting clothes. They had blindingly white smiles. They gave every "h" following a "w" more attention than it deserved. Everyone moved to an extravagant Busby Berkeley choreographed production. The set was designed by Norman Rockwell. The music was scored by Aaron Copeland. Apple pie and ice cream were served by cheerleaders on roller skates at a drive-in movie theater. All this took place during Easter Sunday. In the middle of the fairgrounds. After I scored the game winning touchdown during the state championship football game. For most of the dream I was trying to look up the skirt of my high school girlfriend. We were holding hands. We were skipping through a field of clover with one more year of high school left. There would always be one more year of high school left. No matter how much time I spent here.

I woke up. I wanted to shoot myself in the head. I wanted to see the insides of my head splattered against the wall. I wanted to send my whole self into nothingness for eternity—to never think another thought again. Never mind. That was an overreaction.

I don't know if I'm poor. I'm pretty sure I am. I almost have no money. Yet I had things. I had money in the past to buy them. I had a decent wardrobe. I didn't look poor. I was well educated. I didn't sound poor. I had people who were willing to lend me money. I owed a lot of money. I was worse than poor. I was supposed to have been successful. It didn't happen. It wasn't happening. I could not figure out why. Maybe I went insane. Nobody bothered to tell me. How polite. I applied to all the jobs I was qualified for. I applied to jobs I wasn't qualified for. I applied to jobs

I was over qualified for. I didn't get any of them. All of a sudden, for no apparent reason, I was poor. I was no longer a meaningful member of society. I must have done something. I was unaware of it. I was either completely insane, or I was merely unsuccessful. Regardless, they treat you the same.

Drawing from my last session, I took solace in the fact that my window staring was improving. Lately, my thoughts drifted to the time I was working. I would think about work incessantly. Even when I wasn't at work. Especially when I wasn't at work. It detracted from everything. It distracted me from philosophical thoughts. And now I was thinking about thinking about spending too much time thinking about work when I wasn't at work. That made me even more upset. Thinking about work had kept me up at night. It still did. It was taking my life. I had nothing to show for it. Too angry to think. Too tired to harness the energy generated by my anger. I had been stuck in this purgatory for so long. I could not remember when or how it began. There was always one thing missing from the equation to set things right. But what was worse: missing a piece of the puzzle or knowing you were missing a piece? Was it the same thing? Why would it matter if it was?

Small people do small deeds because history has cut their story short. Big people do big deeds because history allows it. If a hero dies after the first series of trials and tribulations, they aren't a hero. They were the little person who was always a schemer who got what they had coming to them. History chooses.

I noticed that my lover who was not my lover started cooking again. She started cooking for me. I stopped cooking for myself. I was becoming dependent. An innocent bystander would assume this was a generous gesture. However. Her new approach to cooking resembled fattening a prize pig for slaughter. I was the prize pig. All the food was rich and fatty. If not delicious. My gluttony thanked her. My paranoia drew attention to the wildly disproportionate portion sizes between us. At times she claimed she would eat hers later. She never did. Whenever I could amass enough energy to exercise, she would protest, "Just stay in with me tonight and be lazy." She was better at making excuse about exercise than I was. I started to gain unsightly weight. I started to piece together aspects of her scheme: if I became less attractive, she would have more control over the relationship. If we broke up, I would no longer be able to return to the single's market and replace her with a younger, more attractive version. If I had a heart attack, she would heroically save me. She would become my emergency contact. She would be welcomed back into the operating room as "family." Once in the operating room, she could plant devices inside me. Tracking devices. Devices monitoring fidelity. Etc. The doctors would be in on it. I could never let on that I knew her scheme. I attempted a significant reduction in consumption. This plan failed immediately. To get more exercise, I started to walk faster when we went out. This confused her and the general public. It became obvious that I would have to resort to my own scheme to make her less attractive. I would start providing purposefully misguided feedback on hair, make-up, outfits, shoes, etc. Of the very few people I still knew in the area, these simpletons found her very attractive. I thought she was remarkably average. I would start spreading rumors: "Underneath her make-up she is downright ugly." I think I was starting to fall in love with her.

It was a rainy day. I hardly realized. I hadn't been staring out the window for a while now. Instead, I had been staring at the television set. I hadn't processed any of the images. I couldn't stop thinking about the past. My superiors' had provided me with an infantile scolding. I missed a deadline. I had no control. My mind still needed to gain the satisfaction of proving its case to a jury of no one for the millionth time today. This entertainment would not pacify. Instead, choosing what to watch became its own burden. I was reminded of something I heard recently. Successful individuals live efficiently. Limit your wardrobe to one or two items. This saves time and mental energy. The ability to let something go. Or capture it and build it into an organizing principle; i.e., a set of laws, an art form, a scientific formula; i.e., a representation from which to build and generate meaning; i.e., to project both into the future and onto the past, to write the future and the past at once, something to stamp the past, present, and future; i.e., to make time itself with.

I was struck by the notion that this struggle permeated everything. It could be used to explain everything. Every individual's life. Every culture since the beginning of time. Every religion. Every academic school of thought.

Not having anywhere to go with that thought, I went to my closet. I started to get rid of clothes I had never worn. I told myself I might wear this someday. "Someday" meant "never." I made a mental note of this. I didn't narrow my wardrobe down to one or two items. I did remove many items. I would have never worn them. Who was the me who believed I was going to? Another person. Acting and reacting to dead motives. And by speaking the words, I actively singularized my narrative. For whom?

My lover who is not my lover has become more and more unbearable. Or more bearable. I will know more tomorrow.

I am stuck inside my life. It is claustrophobic. Could I bear an eternal Being? If my life was something other than this one dimensional purgatorial moment. Instead, I was living moments constructed by the lives of others. They appeared to be living their lives. Not merely stuck inside them. Perhaps I am stuck inside my life because I have made every decision incorrectly. I only know what not to do. That is all I have ever done. I have no idea what I am doing. Aside from slowly losing the motivation to do anything. I don't want to do anything. Nothing brings me joy. Nothing excites me. The only thing that kept me going were my highly delusional dreams. Now those are fading. All the doubts that everyone has ever had about me are true. Every step is a step further away from an original goal that is forever lost. Everything is a lie to help me forget. I am a million miles from everything. I can no longer tell if I'm even trying. I can no longer tell if I too have started to cash in. I'm betting against me. If I keep being underappreciated, at least I know I'm right. The fight. An overwhelming inevitability. A force I cannot see. It is everywhere. Pushing against me. It might be the only thing molding me together. Perhaps I shouldn't protest too loudly. This has become a bitter pill. In previous years, I used to say: "Bite the hand that feeds you. It is getting in the way of your food." I wouldn't take advice from me.

A deluge of news reports. Our newly elected President will execute a more aggressive war strategy. I didn't know that was an option. We were already in constant total war. With ourselves and with others. Aggressively. But the news will say anything. Politicians will say anything. The information could be false and the war could still be real. Or they could both be false and people could still be dying for something they believe is real. Either way, the war was not on my front doorstep. Which was not my front doorstep, it was a rental. Which begs the question: whose side was I on? Was I only renting my allegiance? My lease was up soon. I was behind on rent. I didn't have a job. I didn't even like my apartment. Some rooms had their moments. None of this was sustainable.

The path of least resistance should be taken if the path of most resistance doesn't have a return policy.

I have been separated from my life path. I am considering the possibility of reincarnation. I keep living the same life over again. It will only stop until I live it perfectly. I make different decisions every time. These decisions lead me down different paths. I have to trust certain instincts. Can I ever know if I keep living this life over again? Maybe I live it the same way every time? Maybe I make the same mistakes every time? Maybe I am waiting for a time when I do something different? It doesn't matter if I see it through till the end or choose it to end early. Either way it re-sets. I can never know how or why. Am I alone? Everything that surrounds me is an elaborate lie. Humanity's historical context, my future, etc. What's the point of the lie? Who stands to profit from this elaborate hoax?

Have an in-depth conversation with someone right now.

In the past. I remember when I slept through my alarm clock. At the time, I was growing suspicious. Was this the handiwork of my non-lover? Did she turn off my alarm clock? I was late for work. Did I hate her or love her more? Was she providing me a challenge to overcome and become a stronger person in the process? My superiors were not pleased. The exact time I arrived never mattered. Nothing depended it. As long as I wasn't obscenely late and didn't fall behind the work load. It was simply a number that someone at some point had arbitrarily decided. It was simply an opportunity for my superiors to not be pleased. And so they weren't pleased. Like clockwork, they regurgitated phrases from a pamphlet that must have been titled, "What to Say When an Employee is Late Because This is Bad." I had always known there was no justice in this world. However. My brain perpetually overrode this command. I continued adhering to vaguely sketched moral boundaries. This was an ever-replenishing source of disappointment. What's worse, I continually caught myself attempting to impose my own sense of justice on the world. This has been cast within the only mold it has ever found itself encrusted: forms most unusual and backward as possibly conceived. While waiting in line. I'd stammer indignantly. Others ignored what should have been an iron clad social order. No matter how false it was. I still operated with an impenetrable sense of cause and effect. The same cause and effect I mock on a regular basis when applied by others. There is no way out. There is no choosing what one is. One is what one is.

Modernity's mental state is the blurred line between perpetual paranoia and a healthy consideration of multiple possibilities converging to protect your best interests.

Disclosing your romantic intentions to another person presents an insurmountable dilemma. Your first instinct is the honest reveal: "I want to be with you," "I need you," etc. However. This automatically infers a lack: you have needs that are not satisfied. As is the current proper custom, the target of your affection will justifiably develop the following line of inquiry: "Why doesn't this person already have this need satisfied?" This naturally raises the question: "What is wrong with this person?" Therefore, it is perfectly sensible (following the current proper custom) for them to conclude: "There must be something wrong with this person, as they don't already have another person to fulfill this role in their life." This is why individuals who already have partners have seemingly endless opportunities for more partners. It is why as soon as you have a partner, others become attracted to you. If you already have a partner, you also don't notice the lonely in-between time of not having a partner. Therefore, the best way to be a single person on the dating scene is to already have a partner.

The still early morning. A vacant world with its light fog lifting. Clarity provides a hint of pine wood. A dewy sea of golfing grass. On the other side of the fence, a breeze blows the musty hay golden to meet the sun. All for me.

In the end, I am left with nothing. Therefore, I write about it. Therefore, I have something. It is mostly nothing. This remainder, an inadequate justification occurring long after the fact. When there is nothing to be done. I wonder what leads me to believe my life is worth recounting. Even recounting to myself. The existence of the universe. And the story of my life. Side by side. It makes it difficult to consider me. And I am me. But it's all I have. And so it becomes the universe once again. I remember previous justifications. The unusually rapid oscillation between my self-importance and self-doubt. This allowed me to believe. I was interesting. But like everyone who has come before me, I was pissing-out platitudes as parables. I didn't think anyone would notice. They notice. I didn't notice until now. Everyone notices everything. Always. Especially when you suspect they don't. That is the instant they notice most. Like sharks to blood. They hate you for it. They've always hated you for it. Sorry if that makes you self-conscious. Never mind, forget what I just said. It's only me who has these problems. I am transparent. I am a master of none. I sit and type. There is no audience. There never will be. Yet, I type. My superpower is fooling myself into believing there is an audience for my work. Just long enough to complete my work. Just long enough to motivate me to do my work. While simultaneously knowing there is no audience. While living with this truth. While I type. It is difficult work. Nobody will stumble upon these dinosaur bones. Nobody will reconstruct them with added value for everyone's amazement. "How were these brilliant ideas overlooked?!" Will say nobody. Nobody will assassinate anybody. Nobody will start a world war over these haphazard ramblings. So at least there's that. Perhaps that is more important. It's not the people you influence, it's the people who ignore you who matter most.

I was owed certain things. I had done certain things. This was passing through my brain space as I stood waiting for the bus in half-dried jeans. To begin with. When I arrived at the laundromat, I was wearing the only pair of mildly clean shorts left in my apartment. Possibly the universe. I didn't have time to check. Time had passed. Next, I changed in the laundromat bathroom. I changed into what I thought were clean, dry jeans. I did this to engineer the image of a somewhat respectable adult. I figured I would dress as a somewhat respectable adult in case there was someone on the bus worth impressing. I'm an idiot. Life was a check-list. A series of grand logical steps with smaller missing connections. School? Check. Set-backs? Check. Axe to grind? Check. Because of this, so this. I knew there was no one running the show. There was no right and wrong. There was no justification for anything that happened. Yet, I didn't act with this knowledge. I acted as I always acted. I acted as I never learned from the crushing disappointment generated by trusting an underlying overarching logic. But somehow, out of the randomness of the cosmic chaos, some superior lifeform had created fast food. Why did they do this? I will never know. My questioning stopped. Fast food was the answer to everything. For the time being. I finished eating. Back at my apartment. I felt accomplished for no apparent reason when I put away the rest of my laundry. Mission accomplished. It's the small things that matter most—I could imagine a hack-writer writing here.

I came up with a new word the other day: knowthing. It means "know nothing" or "to not know anything."

I was drunk on an airplane. I thought of a brilliant idea for a story I was writing. I got out my notebook. I couldn't find my pen. The idea was escaping me. Where on earth and air did I put my pen? I got up quickly. I stumbled to the back of the plane. There was a flight attendant with an immaculately pressed uniform. Thank the _____ (insert airline) gods! My words formed a question about a pen at him. He lisped back at me, "Um, sir. You have one. It's behind your ear." In a daze, but somewhat relieved, I reached up. This clever sky wizard had placed a pen behind my ear. Embarrassment hung behind an oversized smile. "Thanks! This... this really helps me a lot. I needed this." I returned in a hurry back to my seat. I completely forgot what I was going to write. Was I really that drunk? Yes. And no. I could have forgot about the pen if I was sober. I do stupid stuff when I'm sober. Also. Get over yourself. It wasn't that stupid. Think about the you who put your pen behind your ear. Think of all the things that happened between that moment and the moment that the you who needed your pen couldn't find it. Did you really stand a chance of remembering where you put it? With your glasses on, could you feel a pen behind your ears? Don't be so dramatic. But still. You are also really drunk. Regardless. I appreciated the professional courtesy the sky wizard showed towards a drunken bumbling idiot. Obviously I was not the first drunk who had lumbered down the isle. All serious. Hell bent. Mission oriented. But I was probably one of the first who wasn't rudely demanding more alcohol.

I felt an enormous weight. The pressure. To watch my life pass by without acting within it. Spending this decade hoping I will enjoy the next. So I felt no enjoyment. And the years flew by. No. Maybe the years dragged on? I can't tell. The worrying about worrying about worrying. Etc. This was starting to become a problem for me.

Things needed to add up. Long after I found out they wouldn't or couldn't. I found out. I had filled in narrative gaps with my own delusional fantasies. Only to find. I hadn't. I had been exactly right about everything all along. This was worse. Well, not exactly right about everything. I was right about the main points. Or am I just deciding what the main points are? After the fact. Cherry-picking the results. Back to nothing. I couldn't even get these quarters to add up. I was two quarters short. The drier gave up on me. The time I allotted. It wasn't enough. I had it down to a science. Science fails. The drier and I had known each other for so long. Typical. The gas station next door wouldn't break a twenty for me. I spent the rest of the day with a pocket full of quarters slamming against my leg to warn the universe I was approaching from light-years away.

I was back at the store. Our President who was not my President issued another decree: today was a romantic holiday. Another one of many. A ludicrous ploy to boost consumer sales. My non-lover did not share this perspective. I was required to purchase a gift. I was required to perpetuate a relationship I did not particularly want to perpetuate. I found myself in the greeting card section of the store. All of them were shit. At the very bottom were a handful of cards haphazardly shoved into the display case. They appeared homemade. An act of subversion? I could only hope. I read the first one, "I could like you forever." This was perfect. There were more: "I like you. (inside of card): Even when I'm not drunk," "You're Alright. (inside of card): So I'm either attempting to reassure you that you're going to be all right, or I'm drawing attention to the fact that you're an incredibly average human," "I'd marry you. (inside of card): If it wasn't such a horrible idea," and "We should make a baby. (inside of card): In five years when the sex isn't as much fun, and we've put on a bunch of weight due to work related stress, stress from our relationship, and from our unhealthy lifestyle." These cards were perfect. My non-lover would not share this perspective. I purchased a card. It was an abomination of authentic emotion. She loved it. There were sexual rewards for my inauthentic generosity. This process alone insured the perpetuation of our society. Of our species.

I didn't want to do anything. Where was I to go from here? Nothing interested me. How long would this last? A few more minutes? The rest of my life? I had been so motivated. I had approached so many years with purpose and integrity. Had it all run out? Had I used it all up in those years? Now I would do nothing. Eventually I had to eat and drink or I would die. I thought about getting out of bed. At least, that's where I would start. I decided against it. This happened to me once in the past. Luckily it didn't last long. How long would it last this time? The first time it happened, I remember thinking "What would happen if I never got out of bed? How long before others discovered my new lifestyle? Who would be the first to discover me like this?" At the time I knew the answer: the last people I'd want to find out. Dependably, it would be my superiors. Some deadline was missed. Not me. They would be furious. What actions would society take against me? They couldn't make me get out of bed. Could they? Is it illegal to stay in bed? Is it enough to diagnose me as insane if I wanted to stay in bed? Life is so heavily dedicated to ensure that everyone is motivated. Life is so focused on making sure you care about something. Isn't that oddly suspicious? What is being covered up? Productivity is starting to sound like an addiction. Oh well. What am I supposed to do? Lay in bed all day? I managed to sit up. Baby steps. Throughout the day I managed to do things. The day went by. My life went by. And then I died. Nothing else happened, and I ceased to be productive. Hurray!

There was never a win without a loss. I got dumped on graduation day. My Grandmother died the day we won the championship. I found out my parents were getting a divorce on my 21st birthday. Was I in charge of this? Did I choose this fate for myself? To ask these questions. It made no difference. And, as I suspected at the time, perhaps these were the wrong questions entirely. Once again, I started to doubt if I was even me. I never do the things I actually want to do. Maybe I was simply a voice inside a Being. I had tricked myself into thinking I was controlling this Being. I was merely along for the ride. Me (this small voice inside a Being) was only making sense of everything afterwards. I had become well practiced. I was doing it so quickly. I assumed it was simultaneous. I was ordering everything into a logical sequence and relating it back to the person I thought I was. As best I could. But apparently the connections I was making were erroneous. I had no better insight than others outside this Being. Perhaps worse. I was merely weaving together a story. At points it only happened to correspond to the actions of this Being. When I got something right, I actually got it wrong. I didn't know that I was merely guessing. Only by chance did the external actions match my narration. Like taking the visuals from a film and underlying a musical recording. At some point the two will appear to correspond. Maybe the rest of me was working against myself because it disagreed with me. More likely, it had no idea I existed at all. After all, I would only be one voice among many inside this Being. Instead of an actor in this play, I was only a spectator. Even if I was the main actor, I'd only be imagining a world in relation to the science, philosophy, etc. that others have discovered. All of these discoveries will eventually be proven false. The logics I use only provide illusory access to perceptions of myself that don't exist. Perhaps my perception of cause and effect has severely limited my ability to see that what I am is exactly what I am. Oh well.

I had a chance encounter with romance. Outside the horrendous orbital pull of my non-lover. We went out in the city. There was no evidence of war. During the night I was momentarily separated from my non-lover. Then I saw her. She was everything I wanted. Previously, I failed miserably to court her. She had politely refused, in the perfect way she did everything. Now she saw me. I saw her. She appeared happy to see me. We started talking briefly. It was going surprisingly well. It felt natural. Easy. We never broke eye contact. We were searching each others faces. Then I saw my non-lover out of the corner of my eye. In a strange move of pointlessly stupid loyalty, I cut the conversation short, explaining that I was with someone and needed to get back to them. As soon as I did, I knew I would hate myself. Why did I do this to myself? Why was I this much of an idiot? I would ask myself these questions almost everyday that followed. She was what I wanted. Would I rather make her jealous than make her my lover? No. That's not why I was doing it. Why did I do it? To avoid a melodramatic scene with my non-lover? Out of sheer convenience. I would be inconveniencing my entire existence from that moment forward. Out of the corner of my eye, I thought I caught a look of disappointment flash across her face. She said something to the effect: "Oh, well, you better go find her." If I had the opportunity to play the situation over again, would I ever make the decision differently? Was the situation ever as open-ended as I imagined it to be? She was being nice. She didn't want to talk to me. I never had a chance. I'm giving myself too much credit for my loyalty to my non-lover. But most likely, it is exactly how I remember it. I made a terrible mistake that would have solved all my problems. I perpetually make this horrendously debilitating mistake.

I thought to myself, if this is hell, this isn't that bad. I mean I could get used to this. Trapped within an infinitely receding feedback-loop of mediocrity. At least there are moments of entertainment. Some bright spots. I can keep busy doing this. And that. Okay. This is manageable. It is horrible. But it is manageable.

I am now eating alone at a diner. As told to me by my inner-stage-directions. I can never escape this voice. Especially when acting against it. The waitress said something strange a moment ago. What was it? She said, "You're not alone." What did she mean? Does she work for the government? "Excuse me, what did you mean just a second ago? You said, 'I'm not alone.'" Waitress: "I just wanted you to feel welcome. I said, 'You're not alone, here...' like when you come here to eat. It's a catchphrase. We're suppose to say it to all our customers." I looked at her anxiously. Fairly certain she hadn't included "here" when she had addressed me. This scenario was unfolding in my reality. The worst possible outcome was inevitable. She read my anxiety as anger. She continued: "I was trying to be nice! What's with you?" She definitely thought I was angry. She continued. "Creep!" Okay maybe I deserved that. Still. The whole thing was odd. I wasn't able to drop it for weeks. Several times throughout the following week I considered returning to confront her. Why had she said that? A month went by. She was at the laundromat. What a strange coincidence—the kind of coincidence that only happens in bad fiction. I didn't realize it was her at first. I stole several sneaky glances. I walked up to her, "Hey, what did you mean in the diner, about me being alone?" She pretended not to recognize me for several seconds. This didn't work. Everyone knows all humans are equipped with highly developed facial recognition abilities. Also, we are all horrible actors. She could tell she was doing a bad job. She gave up quicker than she planned, "If you don't get it, you don't get it. Clearly you're not ready to join the rest of humanity." She left in a huff. Without her clothes. A few months passed and my mind had to let the incident go to time. Time took the problem where I had to leave it.

Today it was reported that our President who was not my President had and important announcement: we had won decisive victories in the war. However. It would take an additional effort on behalf of everyone to finally win the war once and for all. I had no idea what any of this meant. I still didn't know who we were at war with. Or if this war was different from the other wars we were supposed to be concerned with. They interviewed "people on the street" who were very supportive of the President's announcement. Others were not supportive. Yet others were undecided. Every year. The news reports that political discourse gets worse. Yet every year, more time and money is spent on political discourse. And people eat it up. More and more. This time they didn't attempt to elect a semi-intelligent President. The people are bored. They must be entertained. The people wanted to see what would happen if they paraded their leadership's idiocy in the light for everyone to see. The people wanted to proudly celebrate their own unapologetic idiocy. The people wanted change. Previously, everything was run by a bunch of idiots in the background. The intelligent diplomatic face of the Presidency was sent in to hide the grand inadequacy with reasonable strategies and solutions. But now the people wanted bloodsport. Now they are getting their money's worth.

My life is merely a game being played by a higher-lifeform. Or I am living a version of my life that has veered drastically from its life path. Regardless, everything I wanted has happened to another original version of my self. Of all these self-versions, this current version has got the furthest off track. Yet for some strange reason, I want this to be my life. This version of my life has become sentient. But it must make way in order for the game to be re-set. In order for my true self to have been lived fully. It is this completely full-life or original version that sets my expectations. Because the expectations are never met, I am perpetually disappointed. The wrong turn I took was quite possibly miniscule and very long ago: fatigue felt and weakness succumbed. I feel it now. I was never me in this life. Yet I still want to be me. Why won't I just let the game reset? What have I become attached to? I am a master of none. I am living this version to be radically undefined. As long as I possibly can be. As long as my sanity will allow it. Or is it too late? Maybe this is why. I make every wrong decision. Now I understood. Why I have never been in the right place. Why I have always been where I shouldn't be. Despite overly simplistic religions. Despite adolescent moral codes. What if there is a very literal and measurable Right Way to live your life? What if there is a very literal and measurable Wrong Way to live your life? How would you be able to discover The Way? How do you find the legend with the correct decisions written down? When we don't make a decision we think we should. We are merely remembering that this path is not The Way. Whether we eternally relive our lives or not. It is the same thing. Every instant is the only eternity we will ever know. From living the eternity-instant previously, we are left with intuitions and doubts of intuitions. I'm trying to figure out what didn't work before. I'm searching for my purpose. My life's work. Everything I've tried before doesn't work. What can I turn to? Religion? No. Philosophy? No. Science? No. Art? No. Entertainment? No. The works of others? No. The government? No. Family? No. Friends? No. Myself? No. Can anything be trusted? No. These apartment windows? Several weeks later I would be struck by an equally debilitating thought: everything is exactly as it seems. Anything that suggests otherwise is a distraction to set me off on the wrong path. Oh well.

Why hadn't the pharmacy completed my prescription? A little voice started engineering a scenario. This incident was not random chance. It had been reoccurring. Hadn't it? I didn't receive my prescription. They wanted me to be unbalanced. I had only been nearly successful. They wanted me to be hungry. I had often woken up in the middle of the night dreaming that I had been working on something. For someone else. A higher-power. Was I doing their dirty work? I suffered mortality. They did not. They needed me. You would have to be crazy to believe that. Exactly what they would want you to think. Insanity would be just another social deterrent they would develop in this game. Another measure of penalization for revealing the game itself. They had somehow arranged my life to make me the most fit to do this work. I'm not sure what I was doing for them in my dreams. I woke up exhausted. I woke up feeling like I should have been paid.

These thoughts troubled me for some time afterward. What would these galactic overlords look like? Maybe they didn't look like anything? They were something like pure energy. They were concepts like religion, hunger, or football. We do their bidding. What would the life of a concept look like? Could they have sex? Would I rather be one of these higher-powers or would I rather be me? Maybe the concept of myself was already one of these Eternal Galactic Super Beings? Maybe we all are. Or only famous people. I don't feel like an Eternal Galactic Super Being, so I doubt that's true. These thoughts came back to me when I was holding a baby the other day. Don't worry, I didn't steal this baby. It was my niece. I suppose this would actually make it easier to steal her. But I didn't. I don't want you to think I'm strange. I was holding my niece. We comfort babies when they are upset. Maybe these concepts like science, success, or symmetry (just to stick with some "s" concepts for now) treat us lower lifeforms in a similar manner: they comfort us when we are upset and anxious. However, similar to a baby in the arms of an adult, we only have a vague notion of what is comforting us. And we certainly don't understand their world—the power they have and the limited capabilities we have. I remember a time when I made coffee and caught the bus for work. I spilled coffee on myself after I burnt my tongue. The coffee was too hot. Work was all right.

However, what if babies aren't like this at all. Perhaps they have an infinite knowledge of all things. They aren't ruled by the nonsense we incessantly and habitually subject ourselves to: rules of language, professionalization, rivalries (real or imagined), failure and success (real or imagined), etc. Just because babies cannot communicate their findings doesn't negate the existence of said findings. On the contrary, they cannot communicate their findings, so they spend more time discovering answers to important questions and less time bothering to communicate them. The grown up world is so obsessed with communicating every little detail of what we know that we have stopped knowing anything.

I was half asleep. A small creature ran up my back. I sprang out of bed immediately—simultaneously throwing off my shirt and in the same motion hurling it against the wall. A scurrying spider resumed its crusade toward my bed (an abyss of sheets and crannies). I had seconds to react. I quickly weaponized my shirt. With the help of the floor, I made short work of the spider's existence. Without delay, guilt set in. My instantaneous reasoning replayed itself for my viewing displeasure: "This spider might be poisonous. No time to check. It's either me or you. One of us has to go, spider. And I'm going to make damn sure it's not me. I have to draw the line somewhere." The strike was preemptive. It was unjustified. I acted on an astonishing lack of information. There were a multitude of alternative responses. It was only a spider. But I was horrible. As every other horrible person. On a smaller scale. It was the same action. The same motive. The same thought process: defensive offense. The hypothetical victim became the real killer. Everything is justifiable after the fact. Anything to survive. Better me than them. I never killed another spider. For a couple years.

Only an idiot will stop at nothing to appear intelligent.

Over and over. Revolutions. My laundry in the dryer. If we keep living the same life over again, then as babies, we are actually closer to the peak of our knowledge. Babies are closer in age to our previously-old-selves. But through all our new struggles we forget the life we've previously led. We live it over again. Some people have lived their life-loop many more times than others. They will be more practiced. They overcome obstacles we can't even see. This is what differentiates wisdom from knowledge. I've lived this life-loop a few times already. That's why I sense the game is rigged. But I can't tell if I am wise, or if I am merely knowledgeable, or if I am the stupidest person who has ever existed. It certainly feels as if all of this has happened a million times before. When something bad happens, it doesn't really surprise me. I should have seen it coming from light-years away. Yet I forget. I'm not baby-smart yet. Just then the bus driver turned on the radio. A song mentioned "baby" in a very different context.

Sleep is impossible. When I do fall asleep, my dreams are incredibly vivid. I'm either punching the time clock for these higher-lifeforms (I still can't tell if they are pure energy or the concepts we are enslaved to), or I find myself in the most bizarre yet seemingly normal situations. These situations are seemingly normal because when I hear myself describing the dream out loud, they sound as boring as the dream stories I automatically tune out when others attempt to share them with me. As they corner me in the elevator. But since I've already started, I'll continue. I fell asleep watching an educational documentary on physics. Later, I dreamed that what researchers had thought was our consciousness or soul turned out to be the smallest particle of matter in the universe. While we are made up of millions of particles, our Being (that controls everything) can be located in this, the smallest and most fundamental particle. When I die this particle retreats back to its impossibly small dimension. My other particles go elsewhere. But I go there. Until I become something else again. Perhaps I merely remain myself within this smallest particle. I wonder what it's like to exist as a consciousness particle. I hope the parties are fun. The particle defied detection for so long because it was cruising through our quantum cities at speeds undetectable by our quantum police officers and their radar guns. To reach this particle one has to venture out to the very edge of our multi-multiverse. If we travel down to this microscopic world, we would travel up into the outermost reaches of space. I'm sure we would be able to see our galactic-superpower-overlords at some point along the way. Maybe we could all grab lunch together? Or maybe they are waiting for us at the end of our journey? They will greet us in the vast minuteness of our quantum galaxies where our consciousness resides before we turn back into a baby again.

Later, I reflected on this situation. All I am. A miniscule particle barely holding everything together. All the biological matter that surrounds me. It has taken this "me" particle an eternity to construct and protect. If I died, my soul would remain trapped within this particle. Could I do it again? Or would it take millions of years? What would I be in the mean time? Pure insanity? Why am I cursed with these thoughts? Is my purpose to fully realize these terrifying experiences in order to communicate them to others? Have others thought these thoughts and not been able to hold their biological matter together afterward? Why is my mind taking me to these places? In preparation? To warn others? To alleviate the fear if others stumble upon these thoughts?

Everything haunts me. I have no reconciliation with the past. I can envision no future. The past few years. Fueled by the desperately self-constructed motivations. My path to paradise would be treacherously hellish but worth it. It was not. Nothing became of me. I sacrificed what I was led to believe were "the best years of my life." For nothing. All the hard work. Everything was grossly misguided and ultimately pointless. I would spring from failure to failure. I convinced myself I was building character. I convinced myself I was taking risks to increase my chances of success. It wasn't true. The biggest obstacle to receiving what you want is wanting it. I've never received anything I wanted. Instead. Step by step. Worn down by time. I've merely convinced myself that what I received was what I wanted all along. It doesn't help that a necessary condition of desiring something is the fact that you can't have it.

Lately, I spend most of my time trying to figure out what to do next. Or from the perspective of that fly on the ceiling: I spend most of my time siting in my chair staring at a blank wall.

I remember my friends in the not so distant past. They were not my friends. They were friendship remnants. The profile of the remaining members: competitive business-oriented males. Uncultured. Jealous. Petty. Etc. Complete confidence no matter the question. No matter the answer. They held strong opinions on every discourse. They never shied away from loudly inserting their opinion. Each one of them was the best. Despite evidence to the contrary. So in many respects, we had a lot in common. But there was something very different. What it was? I could never discern precisely. It was fundamental. For starters, this particular brand of male spent an inordinate amount of time and money to dress in a particularly unoriginal and uninspired manner. They considered themselves both analytic and creative thinkers. Because they purchased art. They paid close enough attention in their college courses to convince themselves they could win every debate by sheer will, tone of voice, loud gestures, and overpoweringly premature celebrations from compatriots who declared them the winner. Whoever "won" was always the first to admit "It was all in good fun." They attempted to convince bystanders they were only debating for the sake of debating. It never mattered who won. It always mattered who won. These males are hired through a familial connection. Their children will glide through the world on familial connections. Meanwhile, they will constantly fail to understand why others can't simply pull themselves out of poverty. After all, they succeeded without any help. If you don't consider all the help they received. Most nights I was able to drink myself into having a lot of fun around them.

I don't understand. After all these years and disappointments. I operated as if life was a worthwhile endeavor. How do we get rid of all expectations? I remember a particular day several years ago. I expected that my car would start today. I was running late for work. It did not. I had to wait for the bus again. I expected it would arrive. It did not. I wasn't able to go to work today. I was upset until I remembered: I don't like going to work. I hate my job. I never want to go again. Luckily, I got my wish. I got fired. So I had to find a new job to hate. More than hating my job, I hated finding a new job. So, as they say, "Everything works out in the end."

When I was younger I was seized by the realization that eventually I was going to die. It was an overwhelming sensation. I never feel it anymore. What else don't I feel? I wonder if babies are the opposite. Are they seized by the realization that they are alive? Does this startle them? Does this provide them with the same anxiety? Now, I almost welcome death. I say almost. A couple of seconds, minutes, days, weeks before I die, I will receive wonderful news. Or I will meet the love of my life. Or I will receive a large sum of money. Something spectacular will happen. And then I will die. The higher-powers would never let me die when it would be the most appropriate time to fade into the nothingness. No, they are a cruel bunch. They must be entertained.

Modesty is the lowest form of lying.

I have a reoccurring dream wherein I can't stop talking about my reoccurring dreams. In fact, I still might be in one now. In yet another type of reoccurring dream, my teeth start falling out, or they ache, so I pull them out. Some primordial fear come back to haunt me. Everything haunts me. I said something dumb last night when we were out for drinks. It haunts me. I doubt anyone heard me. It still haunts me that I said it. My tooth exodus could be interpreted as the manifestation of an unconscious lack of control over my life. Duh. Or the very conscious lack of control over my life. The last few times I've pulled out my teeth in a dream, I did it to prove I was dreaming to whomever was accompanying me. I'd wake up shortly thereafter. I've attempted to pull my teeth out when I'm awake, but alas, they do not budge. This is not a dream. For now. Say what you want about being awake, at least I've got a mouth full of teeth. This is bound to change.

Are there any other tests I can do to see if I'm trapped in a deeper sleep-state? The obvious one: kill myself. The stakes seem a bit high. Maybe they aren't? No, they are. Maybe they aren't? No, they are. Etc.

My lover who was not my lover thought we needed a vacation. I told her, "I doubt it's safe to travel because of the war." She looked at me as if I was crazy. I assumed it was safe to travel. Or she was trying to kill us. She knew I planned to spend this time looking for a job. She had a job. She started paying for some of my things. I was becoming indebted. A horrible feeling. Is this what love felt like? She convinced me that I needed to get away. I was grateful. Or I hated her. The vacation was pleasant at times. Other times it was a lot of work. There was a lot of running around—making sure we arrived at places and events on time. I found myself worrying: was I not relaxed and having fun? The lovely backdrop of historic districts, scenic landscapes, highly recommended restaurants, etc. I felt a great anxiety. I shouldn't waste this precious time. Away from my anxious day to day existence.

A man started talking at me on the bus. Since I wasn't given an opportunity to respond, it's doubtful whether we had a conversation. He was simply looking at me while he was talking. When he dropped acid the other day, he felt a sudden overwhelming sense of enormity. He realized how little everything mattered. This life is insignificant. He said he was an eternal particle that transcended space and time. He had morphed into bizarre forms and was let to play over galactic expanses. I listened because I had no other choice. I nodded when he seemed to be looking at me (not just through me). I'm not sure if this confirms or disproves any of my theories.

Fight the battles in front of you. They are aplenty.

Halfway through the one-sided conversation my mind started to wander. I was paying more attention to his gestures than what he was saying. I do this when bored in conversation. It happens more than it should. Eye contact always struck me as a bizarre convention. I can never focus on what someone is saying while attempting to maintain eye contact. I need to separate my sensory experiences. I end up paying more attention to what they are doing visually if I look at them. I end up hearing nothing. Currently, he wasn't making any interesting gestures. Now I was completely bored. Something struck me as important this morning. We are comprised of an infinite amount of infinities. Each occurring in such rapid succession that we can't see the spaces in-between. Like a film reel. They happen so fast that we can't see how each infinity is a separate frame. Each infinity occurs simultaneously: from the beginning of time to right now. Much faster than any measure of time. Our causal connections distract us. They distract us from witnessing eternity playing out from the beginning of time to the present in the blink of an eye. We are perpetually reliving everything that has ever happened to us in order to move forward. We move with the weight of all time on our backs. Our time and the time of everyone else who has ever lived. If we could find a way to listen to all these voices at once, we could find a way out of all the problems we currently face. Our casual causal connections distract us. We are radically disconnected. We have no way to embrace this. I am dying every second. Time starts over from the beginning. I'm alive. I'm me again. Nobody noticed. I don't notice. We have not mastered the slow way. To see the spaces in-between the frames. In-between the constantly occurring infinities.

A naïve and altogether artless public-service announcement. It occurred in a long line of advertisements. They disrupted the television program bringing me solace. The public-service announcement attempted to provide an uplifting message about depression. It made me want to kill myself.

I was revisiting my previous thoughts when I fell asleep watching the physics documentary. We go smaller and smaller with microscopes and bigger and bigger with telescopes. Yet we are unable to make the connection. We are looking at the same thing. We are reaching out to the point where the two will meet (if we can get there before civilization destroys itself). Once we see where the small and big meet, we will slow down the film. We will see the separate infinities on different frames. We will find The View. The View is not another illusion. Like separate nodes on the sound-wave of a beat-boxer, we hear the noises together. They are separate. We can't hear the spaces in-between. The construction. We gloss over the cause and effect. In favor of seeing the cause and effect. We see connections at the expense of being able to see how cause and effect are radically disconnected. We have to see the connections. This motivation is what causes us to see them. It is practiced. Otherwise how would we survive? Send people to the moon? If we lived in the openness, would we live as an Alzheimer's patient? Would we live as a baby without object-permanence (if it turns out that babies are not the genius-overlords I suspect them to be)? Is there another way to live with both? To see the gap in-between the film frames (perhaps through repetition?). How do we see them without cause and effect? Without measurements and calculations? The answer can't be more measurements? Can it? More science? More religion? More more? How could that possibly be the way to achieve anything worthwhile? If science, religion, philosophy, history, economics, democracy, art, literature, etc. were supposed to solve our problems, shouldn't they have done it by now? What would another kind of living look like? How would we sustain and thrive without measurements and calculations?

How do we see the gaps? The blank spaces in-between. Through glitches in our everyday lives? Mistakes, jokes, paradoxes allow us to envision our reality as construction. The View of the constructed nature of everything. Not just the major distraction of cause and effect. Any current explanation of the universe isn't The Way. Therefore, every explanation only works as a distraction. Any way of making money is a distraction from The Way. Anything ever published is not The Way. No school of thought has ever come close to understanding The Way. Pursuing The Way itself will disqualify it from being The Way. No way that has been thought is The Way. If we found The Way, there would be no need for anything else. There would be no other thoughts. There would be no need to write. There would be no theory of The Way. The Way is the thought that leads to no other thoughts. The Way is a death in life. It needs no elaboration, no system, no next step. It does not need to be expressed. Am I writing a riddle for my future self? I have no answer. Now. I keep writing. If I had found The Way, I would have stopped. Now. The most profound thought needs no accompaniment, no ornamentation, no elaboration. Etc.

I'm the most agreeable when I'm the most artificial.

This practiced cause and effect leads us to believe in overarching narratives that tie ourselves and our universe together. Don't other Earth Beings believe they have tied their universe together? Yet, we assume we have achieved much more than, say, sea anemones and flightless birds. We believe we are more intelligent. But simply using more of the same logic (developed to the nth degree) isn't much of an improvement. What do the higher-galactic Beings think of our self-appointed superiority? Do they laugh at us? The overarching narratives we tell ourselves and others help us practice the cause and effect necessary to put people on the moon. Perhaps. They do not help us obtain world peace or discover a way of governing that allows everyone to live happy, fulfilling lives. Isn't that curious?

The man had stopped talking at me. Had he asked me a question? How should I respond? I searched his face. I searched the reactions of passengers next to me. I searched my own motives. I searched the perceived consequences of every action I had ever taken. There appeared to be no expectation for me to respond. He glanced at me. I nodded. This seemed to be all that was necessary...all that was necessary to convince him to ramble on. Unfortunately. When reflecting on what just occurred, I had a difficult time discerning my own musings from the narrative of his acid trip. Had his thoughts infiltrated my theories? Perhaps. I only assumed I had tuned out his conversation at me. Instead I was following along. Only slightly behind. Only slightly copying everything he said. I convinced myself it originated from my own head. I could not completely dismiss this outlandish implausibility. Lately. My life had been frequented by these moments. Moments that failed to be completely verified or rejected. Or was I just becoming more aware that life is made up of moments that fail to be completely verified or rejected? One time an ex-girlfriend told me I had behaved rather badly when our cohort had gone out for drinks after class. She was already upset with me. The other night I tied one on with close friends. I only half believe in the severity of my infractions. Furthermore, she had also been drunk. Probably the most drunk I had ever seen her. Yet at the same time, I couldn't completely dismiss what I had done. She may have been right all along. There was no authority on the matter. I asked members of the cohort about the evening. None of them had strong opinions. Nor did they seem to care. Nor could they remember anything clearly. The technology that helped record the evening offered no deciding information. My past experiences couldn't either. I had been a bastard while drunk. I had also been perfectly well behaved. My past and current emotional state offered no clues. I had no connection to the motives ascribed to the situation painted by the perception of others. There was no perspective that could hold the event. What had actually happened was lost to time. It could have as easily happened as not. Life is surprisingly full of these moments. Neither of us had a foundation to base our opinions. I continued to defend myself. She continued to attack me. We didn't last long. I imagine these baseless battles are common in most marriages. We are a disgusting species.

Sometimes, during the first stages of sleep, I can pull back from the narrative that is occurring. I ask myself, "Do I actually know the characters involved? What is this narrative referring to?" When this process of questioning occurs I can work backwards. The narrative and the characters start to dissolve. Now fish out of water. There isn't any supporting material for them to survive in. Once the first level of associations breakdown, everything starts to go. In waking life, associations are repeatedly reinforced by other factors. "I know so-and-so because they do this-and-this. They know this other person and we had these experiences together." In waking life there is a function that perpetually provides another level of associations once the previous level breaks down. Imagine falling down an infinite elevator shaft. A safety net is released at every floor. If the safety net fails, another will be deployed at the next floor. But what would happen if this system failed in waking life? What would it mean if the same breakdown in narrative and logic would happen in waking life? What would make the system break down? What would it be replaced by? Would society function better without narrative and logic? Would society function at all? Through evolutionary processes, are our brains instinctively hard-wired to make these narrative associations? To rely on this infinite elevator shaft of safety nets? This is what I was pondering, a few years ago, while waiting in line at the bank during my lunch break. My lunch break was short. The bank line was long. My bank account was small. The gentleman in front me very large. Surely he wasn't using all the fat in his calf "muscle." It was the size of my head. It's a good thing they don't have cutlery at banks. I might have tried to make a quick snack of it. It would have saved me some money. I'm sure the bankers would understand.

I started to consider other instances. Right before I've fallen asleep. I'd catch myself stressing about situations and people I've never known. Where do these thoughts come from? Do other lives inhabit my consciousness? Do the narratives of other main characters work through me? In other time periods? In other dimensions? Does the push and pull of our narratives effect each other? Do these narratives have physical properties? Do they behave in calculable ways like the laws of gravity? In waking life there is a gravitational push and pull to our narratives. There is a social gravity in waking life. We are attracted to certain narratives and cultural norms. We can measure the probability at which individuals gravitate toward certain beliefs. We can measure how they will act in certain situations. Do the decisions I make in my waking life effect these other lives connected to me via the dream world as well? It would make sense. They have been doing major damage to my life. Perhaps it's revenge. Perhaps I've been unknowingly doing damage to their lives? How would I be able to figure this out? The bank line refused to move. So I returned to work. Hungry. No succulent calf meat. Thanks, people in other dream dimensions.

Back home I realized something. It had been occurring in the background for a long time now. My obsessions helped hide my overwhelming de-pression. As long as both my obsessive nature and my depressive nature were working at full tilt, they would cancel each other out. Well, for the most part. Almost. They jousted. More or less. However, over the past few years, my motivation started to wain. I no longer had what others would deem to be positive/normal goals. I no longer had my deadlines to obsess over. It became abundantly clear. I was merely obsessive. I would obsess over anything that came under my radar. Once realized, I became more depressed. The projects were no longer obsessive in a way that was beneficial or fulfilling. That's when the depression started to bleed over into both sides of the equation. No obsession over a project was there to lift me out. No obsession was there to help me forget. But at least I was feeling something! This thought was not as comforting as I hoped it would be. It made me more depressed.

I hear gunshots. Every night outside my rundown apartment. I keep thinking the war has reached homesoil, but it is simply the poverty driven crime that fuels the violent outbursts. Not everyone is poor. There are quiet a few rich people who live in the area. But the rich and the poor are almost evolving into two different species. They exist on two different levels of consciousness. They have two different realities with which they live in the world. However. They both come together in their bizarre support for our idiotic President who is not my president. Rich or poor, stupidity is a great uniting force.

It was nighttime. I was staring aimlessly at the floor. I almost had the answer to everything. Maybe it was nothing. I shot out of my chair wondering why this should happen to me right now. In my living room. In my shoddy apartment. Those thoughts started to distract me from the moment of brilliant inspiration. The answer to everything had come too fast. I didn't understand its logic. I only glimpsed it. I started to doubt if it made sense. "No." I told myself. "I understood. Stop doubting yourself for one goddamn second." In the end, it made no sense to me at all. Even if I could re-think it. Even if it was written out in front of me. I would not understand. The answer to everything might as well be right in front of us every day of our lives. But doubting what we know to be true is what makes the whole thing run. Probably. So it wouldn't matter. There must be many logics much more radical than our own. We keep searching for them, but we are using our own useless logic. What else can we do? How do we pull back the camera to see our logic as one of many others? Perhaps through repetition? Clearly not through analogy. It would be strangely comforting to know I am stabbing wildly at the night. That I am wrong about everything. Finally, I wouldn't be alone. I realized I was pacing around the room. As if I was some genius thinker. What a phony. "Sit back down and stare at the floor." I thought to myself. I did this until I heard a knock at the door. Late-night party-goers. They were all very drunk. They were all ready to enter my apartment. "Steve's Place!!!????" "Oh, no I think he lives a little further down the hall to the left." "Right on man, you should join us. This chick is crazy." He pointed at no one in particular. "Oh that's all right, I've...I've got some work I should do." I should have joined them. I didn't have any work I should do. I had nothing to do. I really hate myself.

I was struck by the banality of my death. In all likelihood. Death was going to be as banal an event as any other event in my life. It was going to come and go. Just as my life came and went. Without explanation. With a multitude of loose ends yet to be tied up. With no justification. With everything still left unresolved. In short. A complete mystery that would be lost to time. Eternally. I need to get more toilet paper at the store.

I had somehow acquired the habit of attempting to predict my own death. Everyday. Frequently. Throughout the day. It was incredibly annoying. Mildly distracting. Downright morbidly disturbing now that I'm reflecting on the frequency with which it occurred and the situations I imagined it occurring within. For some reason, when I failed to correctly predict my death, when the scenario I had been playing out in my head turned out to be fantastical and highly imaginative, when the fear and anxiety subsided, this did not appear to be a good enough reason to abandon the practice altogether. Even in the midst of doing it, I knew it was ridiculous. Yet, I persisted. However. Perhaps my strategy wasn't crazy after all. By making the situation ridiculous, perhaps I was preventing the reality from becoming real. Regardless. The constant worrying was probably driving me insane. I'm sure the constant possibility or reality of war didn't help. Nor did it help that every individual in our society was fully educated on the multitude of pointless, instantaneous, and arbitrary ways in which one could die on a daily basis. Merely minding their own business. We had a real problem simply keeping people alive who did not want to die on their way to the grocery store. Or the laundromat. Etc.

When we were younger, my friends and I thought we could simply will ourselves into fame and fortune. We attempted to crash old-money upper class parties. I thoroughly enjoyed the puzzled faces worn by the distinguished guests as I scornfully rebuked them, "Don't you know how famous I think I should be?"

Aimlessly standing on my back porch. My life is a study being conducted by higher-lifeforms. They have been trying to figure out why I haven't killed myself yet. With all I've been through. With all the nothing I have to live for. Why on earth (literally where this study is taking place) did I keep going? Previous trial versions of myself had killed themselves much earlier on in the simulation. What made this version of myself continue for so much longer? Perhaps merely the fact that I/he realized so early on that this was a simulation. Perhaps he realized that the only hope of having agency outside the simulation was by beating it. Perhaps this is what keeps him going? Or perhaps he is simply too stupid and stubborn to quit. I still haven't decided if others around me know it's a simulation or if they are programs. Built-in aspects of the simulation. Honestly, I'm impressed. The higher-lifeforms who control the simulation know what they're doing. They can't get me too high or too low. They have suspended me within the prefect anxiety producing purgatory. No wins without a loss. The death of someone especially close would have given me resolve to do great things. It would have brought me to immeasurable lows. It would have raised me to great heights. Getting into trouble. The same thing. Falling madly in love. The same thing. Striking it rich or being completely destitute. The same thing. Life just has to be annoying. Enough. Just enough success balanced with a numbingly consistent and perpetually overwhelming sense of failure.

To perpetually convince oneself to be smart and successful requires an immense amount of concentrated stupidity.

It was becoming increasingly difficult to communicate. Regardless, there was an ironclad attendance policy for my family reunion. One imagines communication skills improving with age. Apparently I was aging in a different direction. From the adolescence of adolescence into the adolescence of old age. The unpracticed observer might consider a not-too distant brief two-year period as my foray into adulthood. It was a foolish attempt to put on the guise of adulthood. It did nothing for me. My whole life I've either been a young boy or an old man. It's the same thing. It makes attending family functions difficult. Pretending to care about the useless small talk of others was impossible. Not caring was freeing. Others, of course, consider it rude. They can't see how you are providing them with an invaluable service. Who else is going to gently guide them to the conclusion that what they are saying is perfectly useless? When else are they going to get a chance to reconsider their pointless life values? Thanks to my services they are able to consider what is actually important to them. Sure, I'm able to play along. Briefly. I just make sure that at a certain point they notice my eyes glazing over. Or that I am gazing off into the distance. Or that my focus has shifted to one of the children kicking a ball around. The overly enthusiastic individual usually wanders off their anecdote: usually a thinly veiled brag about how intense/successful their high-level stock trading career has been. To be clear, I genuinely have nothing against these individuals personally. I'm glad they are doing well. I'm glad they've found something that holds their interest. I'm glad they are excited enough to share it. I want them to share it with someone else. I simply don't have the energy to care. I used to. I don't anymore. This relative of mine is clearly passionate about the stock market. This only reminds me of how far away I am from caring about anything. This only reminds me of how delusional one must be to be passionate about anything. This only reminds me of all the years it takes to become so deeply indoctrinated within a system that one cannot see how utterly pointless it all is. I quickly migrate toward the toddlers or the elderly. Not the children or the 60 year-olds. I seek the refuge of those who recognize how pointless it is to have something to say and somewhere to go. This is my demographic. We get along splendidly. Conversation is minimal and pleasantly vapid. There is a mutual understanding that is immensely deep and remains unbroken throughout the encounter. Nothing is said. In the silence there passes an intensely wise emotional gravity. It is far more rewarding. Rather than energy depleting, it is energy inducing. I leave equipped with the knowledge that if I am bothered by enough relatives next year ("This might be the last time you will be able to see great grandma so-and-so"), I will survive the ordeal. If I have nothing else planned. I won't have anything else planned. Aunt Sybil's potato salad gets worse every year. I think she is losing her mind. Hopefully she will join our circle of castaways soon.

Did you ever stop to think that you are only repeating everything you have always ever said or done and nobody has the decency to tell you? They remain silent out of politeness. Their politeness is allowing you to slowly slip into the most impossible depths of madness imaginable. Hopefully you didn't read this before bedtime. My sincerest apologies. That's what I'd say if I was writing a novel.

I thought about writing to one of my previous professors about a paradox. It was formulated in a conversation I had with myself while taking a shower. But I decided it was insignificant. I'll write it here instead: "Truth is lost through communication." As I thought more and more about this statement, it occurred to me that the more "True" it is the less "True" it is. In communicating this "Truth" to one's audience, an individual must take on the same risk defined by the statement's logic, that is, the impossibility of providing "Truth" through communication. Extending this further, I thought to myself, if the individual wanted to tell the "Truth," they wouldn't have to say anything, it would be understood. Communication distorts, lies, manipulates. It is the point of anxiety that extends us beyond that which we are comfortable. "Truth" is lost through communicating it. Nothing "True" can be communicated. Another statement that defeats its own purpose. As I suspected previously, The Answer or The Way needs no further explanation. If an individual found the one true Answer, they wouldn't need to write it down or think another thought again. It would just be. Maybe this is why toddlers, the elderly, and I sit quietly in silence at these family reunions.

A couple days later I was watching the news. There was a report about a ruthless dictator. At first I thought they were talking about our President who was not my President. There was a piece on a famous ill-behaved starlet. How can some people simply bend the universe to their will? It's never worked for me. Maybe I never really tried? These people never compromise. They never apologize. They have been trained in a special style of mental gymnastics. They are perpetually able to convince themselves they are right when all evidence points in the opposite direction. When grilled by the reporter, the actress always had a comeback. There was always one more way she could justify breaking the rules. My primordial sense of justice led me to believe they would get their's in the end. They never do. They win. They always win. This world does not provide for people who play by the rules this world demands people play by. There are no rules. Until you get caught. Then there are rules. And you should have followed them all along. Shame on you. Somehow I deserved the overwhelming lack of respect from everyone around me. No matter what I did. I must find a way to shed this overarching sense of responsibility and justice. If I am to continue to live in this world. I also need to take the garbage out to the street. Because it is Wednesday.

When I was sweeping my filthy apartment I came up with a new word-question: "a guessing question or to use a question to guess an answer."

Today, when we were out, I overheard my lover who was not my lover describe me as her fiancé. This was somewhat disturbing. I had no rec-ollection of a proposal. Nor did I have any intention of providing one. Furthermore. Later that day. Out of the corner of my eye. I caught the tail-end of a venomous striking glance delivered to a competing female. Better safe than sorry. This was her logic. I assumed she assumed this was a competing female. I was finally starting to realize my situation. I had no idea how "taken" I was. I was not casually dating. Waiting for something better to happen. Anything better was actively being scared away. All over town. On the bus ride home I was really drunk. She said, "You and I were meant to be together forever, right?" Oh shit. There it is. That explains everything. Also, she thinks I am way more drunk than I am. Or rather, this conversation has immediately sobered me up. I had no idea how to respond. How do you say no without saying no? How do you say maybe without maybe sounding like maybe? "Um, I'm not really sure, I guess I've never really thought about it." Considering the circumstances, that couldn't have been the worst response, right? It did not suffice. She persisted. "But if we had to get married, it would be to each other, right?" Well, good for her, I thought. Nobody else has shown this much interest. With the imminent threat of war, how much longer did we have to live? This mediocrity was comfortable. It was much better than the crushing pain of nothingness. The only two options. I played up my inebriation. Or rather, I pretended the conversation hadn't completely sobered me up. In the near future I would need a scapegoat to retract what I was about to say. "Well, I suppose that would be all right."

However. Success can be your biggest weakness. The success of a theory leads to its falsification. The success of a political party leads to its downfall. If a person is too successful at being attractive, the competition to win their love turns into a very strange battle. In this strange battle, the person who is too successful at being attractive won't find genuine love. Their attempt will be sabotaged. Shadowy tactics will be employed by competitors vying for their love. The person who is too successful at being attractive ends up with someone who they do not love at all. They end up with someone who is merely a highly skilled tactician. They end up with a manipulative psychopath. Of course, upon completing their goal, the psychopath will realize their success is completely empty, as they only love the pursuit and the competition. They do not actually want the prize. Idiots believe that the quick-and-easy way to discern the psychopath from the non-psychopath is to filter them out by testing their core-competencies in the areas of family-values, traditional belief systems, and a hearty relationship with god, etc. As if the psychopath doesn't already know that these are easiest ways to win the hearts and minds of the masses. The same holds true for politics. The only way to know for certain if they aren't a psychopath is if they reject family-values, traditional belief systems, and a hearty relationship with god, etc. But then, they might actually be a psychopath. By your standards. Success is yet another way to cleanse something from existence. Success is the universe's way of saying: "Fine, you've been hammering away at this for so long, we will let you have it. However, you are damning yourself." Ants in the jungle are killed by a spore they eat. The spore grows a fungus out of them. The fungi are there to provide balance. To make sure a certain insect doesn't take over the jungle. However, first, the insect must become highly populated before this happens. The insect must first be very successful before it starts to fail on a massive scale. Success is a fungus that kills us and provides balance. Great civilizations don't fall. Great civilizations were never great to begin with. In order to insure that we can start over again, they need to become successful.

Yesterday was hardly a Sunday.

How are we made to care about so much pointlessness? When allowed time to reflect, we know we don't care about so many useless distractions. We know we are going to be fine if we don't get a job, if we get fired from our job, if we don't please our superiors, if something goes wrong. Yet we still feel the weight of the entire world on our shoulders. Maybe the weight holds us together. Perhaps we crave it. But what's the worst that could happen? We could starve to death. Then we would no longer have to worry about it. We desperately hold on to stress and anxiety as if our life depended on them. Maybe our life does depend on them. How can we bypass this process? Not logically, obviously. Through constantly absorbing multiple perspectives? By embodying varied narrative spaces? This thought was interrupted. My upstairs neighbors were loudly making love. Badly. I could tell. He made most of the noise. It ended quickly. The thuds were rhythmless. When the rhythmless thuds ended, she would talk on the phone in the other room. Late into the night. This wouldn't have been so upsetting. If she wasn't so incredibly attractive. He was remarkably bellow average. Entirely. It drove me mad. It was supposed to. It felt purposeful. There was nothing accidental about it. The universe was going out of its way to tell me a joke. It wasn't very funny. It wasn't very original. I had heard it before. Several times. Everyone was going to lose. He was going to be crushed when she divorced him. She was already disappointed that he was who he was. She had managed to make up excuses thus far. It took her two years after the wedding to realize that she had wanted to get married. Just not to him. She didn't have anyone else in mind. Just not him. It turns out. The universe didn't manage to get a laugh or a cry out of me. This was more of the same. So please, universe, try to diversify. However. I suppose you made it into this story, so congratulations, universe. That's what I'd say if I were writing a novel.

Back when I had a job, I called my mother after work. I talked about my job situation. She told me I met so much resistance because I was paving my own way. I never set out to do anything different. I was merely reacting. I was continually on my heels. I was continually fighting off each cascading wave of failure before the next one hit. I was in perpetual recovery mode.

I was in perpetual course correction. I was merely attempting to retreat back to a safe foundation where I could momentarily defend myself from the world. Reside within a sandcastle. I never thought I was asking much. I never thought I was asking for more than anyone else. Actually, I thought I was asking for much less. There were several points when I was content with settling for what I had. But I was never allowed to do that. Had I unconsciously sabotaged myself? Had I tricked myself into taking radical leaps forward? Had I tricked myself into missing the landing? By rejecting norms and my temporarily inadequate situation, I sought to measure my success not by the standards of others but by a metric that has yet to be discovered. This new method would open up a universe of possibilities for others. If only they could understand the radical insights I obtained by not adhering to their customs. It was a great plan. In theory. In practice it never worked. All of my failed attempts at romance. At a career. What if I always gave up too early? Maybe I hadn't been direct enough? I needed to roll for broke. No. The evidence articulates another story. My failure was mine alone. It was complete. I had been actively and consciously rejected. And not just temporarily. They would stand behind their decision. Eternally. There was nothing I could do. Ever. Have they ever told me that they changed their minds? Never. They never call back. They are never wrong. They never apologize. I would never be good enough. I couldn't shake off the feeling. That things could have been otherwise. This was my way of coping. This was my way of becoming the phoenix. Of inventing new worlds. Of rewriting the future history of myself. The sneaking suspicion came back. Perhaps I was in control of everything in my life. So why didn't I give myself everything I wanted? Why did I choose differently than what I thought I ought? I hide the reasons from myself. Then hide the fact that I had a choice. What else was I hiding from myself? At the moment, my slippers. I couldn't find them anywhere in my tiny apartment. The number of places I could put them on or take them off was astoundingly miniscule. They were nowhere to be found. This became the most perplexing problem my existence had yet to encounter.

Go outside. You need more activities.

I had to pay rent. Somehow. The once amicable relationship with my landlord turned sour. Understandably so. At the very least, I needed to pay rent from a few months ago. When he came to collect rent, what was usually a casual conversation about our similar political views had turned into a very terse 'scolding and excuse making session'—that is, when he was able to catch me before I had a chance to slip out. My non-lover suggested I move into her place. It was a trap. A trap with a bottomless pit. I didn't want her to know I knew it was a trap. I made up an excuse. She suggested I temporarily work for her Aunt and Uncle, so I could pay rent. They owned a store. I did not want to be further indebted to her. I was out of options. One morning soon after, I showed up at the store. I had no idea how the place stayed in business. It served no purpose. I looked around. It was outdated inefficiency mixed with cutting-edge pointlessness. I couldn't get a regular job. Yet I would be working for them. It was a Christian religious supply store. This would require an extra phony effort on my part. I lied. About so many things. About my relationship with their niece. About my upbringing. About my values. About my political beliefs. This was easy to do. I was already uncertain about everything. They were nice enough. They were not bad people. Just bat shit crazy. And they were in charge of this whole operation. They made a decent living. The shop was full of works that authors had written in earnest. That publishers and editors had taken seriously. The shop was stocked full of religious icons and statues that took manufactures and artisans serious time and money to make. None of it was high quality. But everything was done very earnestly. And was taken very seriously. After working for a handful days, if I was deep into a work shift, there were moments when I would forget to laugh at my surroundings. I would get lost in the piety of my surroundings. For a second. And then I would laugh. Of course. Her Aunt and Uncle were visibly sorry when my time with them came to a close. They even extended a very generous offer: if another location opened up, I would be first in line for fulltime employment. I thanked them kindly. And for the first time in a long time I prayed. I prayed to god that another location never opened up.

I remember a period in the not so distant past. I spent most of my days actively forgetting everything I had learned. I had spent a lot of time and money on college. It looked good on my résumé. I tried to go to sleep later that night. My mind was racing about worries of the day. My mind was racing about worries of many other days that had come before. I got up to work on a project. As soon as I started, I was overwhelmingly tired. I gave up and laid back down. As soon as I laid down, I was no longer tired. I got up to do work. This went on for the rest of the night. My superiors snapped at me for nodding off the next day. It's a good thing most of us don't possess the dedication it takes to be a genocidal maniac.

I remember the time when I was able to jump-start my car. I took it to a mechanic. He assured me nothing was wrong. I told him there was something wrong. He told me no. I took it home. Now it won't start at all. Now I can't take the car back to the mechanic for him to tell me there is nothing wrong. Nothing is real. I am living in an elaborate game. It must be fun for someone else. I wish it would stop. It doesn't. It never does. Nobody else appears to have the same problems. The people telling me I am good at things are lying to me. Otherwise, if I were as good as they say I am, and as good as I've led myself to believe, I would have a much better career by now. But I don't. So I'm not. No more lying to yourself about systems being rigged. The weight of the projects I want to work on is starting to crush me. These projects were supposed to make a name for myself. I am light-years behind my own self. I will no longer be that person. I will be nobody. Perhaps being a ghost is comfortable? No expectations. No appearances. I'll like being a ghost.

The other night, I planned on going to bed early. Apparently, this did not happen. Instead, I raided my own liquor cabinet—as if I were in high school and my parents were out of town. I polished off a strange and extemporaneous mixture of alcohol. Later, my stomach questioned my motives. I played a strange and extemporaneous mixture of music. Next, I made the very wise decision to go to bed. Just kidding. Of course I went out by myself. I thought I had kicked this habit many years ago. Wrong again. The hard evidence pointed toward a night of fun. My drink receipts. Drunken messages sent and received. To and from a female companion I just met. Flashes of memories: conversations, dance floors, and strobe lights. Of course. Right on time. My guilt. It wouldn't let me celebrate what I accomplished. It provided another interpretation of the evidence. It viewed the night as highly irresponsible. The crushing guilt that I had prossibly (probably and possibly) been rude at times. That I had prossibly made and ass out of myself. That I had prossibly been seen by someone

I knew. This guilt anxiety (guxiety) was thoroughly killing me. I was in a tailspin. Luckily my drunken self knew that my hungover self would be filled with pointless remorse. In black permanent marker I had written on the shitty white linoleum floor of my apartment: "You'll never know where the line is until you've crossed it. Slaves to adventure!" I smiled the entire time I was frantically scrubbing.

You have to be smart enough to follow a specific brand of thinking. You should try to be stupid enough not to understand it completely. This will provide you the ability not to fully buy into it. I was waiting in line at the bank today. I was considering all the bat-shit-crazy ways of thinking I was led to abandon in time. Luckily. What current ways of thinking would I dismiss in the future? The current theory I just now arrived at? I absent-mindedly nodded at a stranger walking by me at the train station. He did not appreciate this. He was some kind of tough guy. He made a threatening gesture. We continued to walk in opposite directions. He yelled. "What you looking at dumbass?" I was unprepared for any kind of emotional response from him. Let alone aggression. This is how idiot dictators win wars. This is how demagogues take power. I did nothing. That appeared to please the aimless aggressor. My nothingness reaction appeared to justify his victory. I briefly looked around to see if anyone witnessed this obscene interaction. My eyes caught those of a professionally dressed woman. I grinned sheepishly. "Wonder what that was all about." There was no shelter at the Inn. She responded. "You're not very popular around here. Are you?" I laughed. I didn't know what else to do. I had no idea what she meant. I was stunned. Not only had she taken a strong stance. She sided against me: the non-aggressor. Furthermore. She sided against the person addressing her. If I had been her, I would have simply nodded my head regardless. I would have agreed with the individual addressing me so that everyone could go about their day. I would have agreed so that no more useless anxiety would have been generated from the incident. However, she saw it as an opportunity to immortalize her opinion in the annals of my future anxieties. Some days are better off not lived. Most days are better off not lived. This past year alone I'd do away with 98% of the days. I'm not even asking to have them replaced by better days. Do away with them completely. Erase them from my mind. So many embarrassing moments. The previous encounter would go away. Forever lost to time.

Last night I had a dream. I was being struck by lightening. I never felt a thing. Before it happened, I heard the warning siren. It was going off in the distant background. I attempted to crawl back toward the glass doors. All I could see. Glass doors. They must have belonged to the brick building. I must have walked out of the brick building before I was struck. The repetition of thought was helping making causal connections. I'm not sure if these connections should have been made. But there was nothing else for me to do. Perhaps someone was feeding me these scenes. They knew beforehand. I would put them together. Just like this. Yes, I was free to put them together. But I wouldn't call that freedom. I was merely attaching the matching parts. Like a daisy chain. As the scenes circled around, I merely put the ends together. I relied on punctuation to guide me. However. It was much more fluid than I wanted to admit. Next time. I'll place the scenes out of order. So long as it doesn't hurt me. Perhaps that is the definition of art: playing with meaning in a way that doesn't hurt you. In the dream, I felt myself sinking into nothingness before forcefully willing my consciousness to return back into the body that lay in bed asleep. I jolted upright. I always return back to this default reality. Possibly a temporary location. Could I will myself out of this body? Into a body somewhere else? I hoped a much younger self. The possibilities would be endless. Life would lay out in front of me like a blank canvas. Like a Saturday morning.

You can have freedom or time. But not both. I have neither. So I write.

The magical worn out VHS tapes of my youth. That was happiness. Now it's the stretching. Stretched into fast-forward or rewind. Now I was stuck. I was still at a bar waiting for the recently met female companion from the other night to show up. A potential romantic encounter. I couldn't believe how meaningless my life had become. Full childhood days at my Grandparents' house. Those days would occupy my thoughts for the entire week. Hopelessly. This isn't living. Life's trick: "Tomorrow, things are going to be different. This night is going to be different." It's never different. Life was barely interesting enough to see what happens next. Nothing was more repulsive than the pursuit of happiness. I found myself worrying about being happy. It was worse than being completely unhappy.

A few weeks later the female told me she couldn't make it. She finally got an audition. It was for a major advertisement. She was really sorry. I told her it was fine. Say what you want about modern technology. At least my slow descent into an almost imperceptible variation of madness will be well documented.

It was Tuesday. But I wasn't sure. I was at the diner again. No waitress. I don't know how this made me feel. I was quickly distracted. Everything I want to happen actually does happen. My sense of justice does prevail. I do get what's due to me. All this takes place in a parallel universe. Not in this one. Somehow the current universe I am living in is the one I have chosen to piece together through cause and effect. This is the logical path I have chosen. This is the version of reality I have chosen. I do not know why. Especially since all the other paths I could have chosen are far more appealing. But I go on. Not knowing why. That is what creates this reality. Not knowing why. I assemble the cause and effects. If I knew, it would no longer be reality. Everything has led up to this. Me not knowing why. That is the reason why. I continue not knowing why. And that is the reason why. Everything continues. If I were to know why. Everything would cease to continue.

I remember the past. I needed advice from one of my superiors. During our meeting in her office, I asked her a pressing question. She attempted to look at me as if I had asked the stupidest question ever. I returned the gaze. Unashamed. Knowing, in fact, I had not asked the stupidest question ever. I asked a good question. I asked a question that I actually needed an answer to. I gave her another look. To signify her failure. Sheer will had not forced me to submit. The assumption that I had made an idiot out of myself did not overtake me. I was well practiced in making an idiot out of myself. I knew I had not done so in this instance. But now I know. Looking back, it's obvious. She was an alien. Everything makes sense. She was sent from another galaxy. To make sure our civilization does not advance past a certain level of intelligence. Therefore, she takes on the corporal form of various individuals in authoritative positions to insure that anyone who might possess enthusiasm does not succeed. Otherwise her behavior is completely unexplainable. She was merely "acting" the role of my superior. She played the part well: a total jackass without any real answers.

I started talking to myself more often. Out loud. And more publicly. Had anyone noticed? Would my lover who wasn't my lover tell me if I was doing this or would she allow this to happen so that I would become more dependent on her? When alone, how loud was I talking to myself? Had I stopped checking to make certain I was alone? Could others hear me? Something else to be overly anxious about. When talking to others, often I forget what I am talking about. When they ask me to clarify what I mean, often I don't have the slightest idea. This has happened a handful of times. I am becoming more or less aware of what is going on around me. Perhaps I always talk without realizing what I am saying. Perhaps all our speeches commence without us knowing where they will end. I am becoming more aware of how we communicate. Or I am showing signs of early onset dementia. Maybe dementia is exactly what I need. Not too much. Just a dash. To loosen things up a bit. To set me free from the world. To expand myself beyond my life. To have one foot in. To have one foot out. I was already on my way. Stepping away from sanity is the only way to understand it. To evaluate it. To check if anyone else is. I've got good news. And bad news.

I remember the time. All at once I felt the sinking weight of impossibility. The impossibility of everything. A person should not feel this. A person should not feel this so early in their life. I don't recommend it. A person should not feel this while they are supposed to give a big presentation in front of so many people that care so much about the topic they are about to present on. I don't recommend it. But that's what happened. Mid-presentation. I didn't care anymore. Not about this. Not about any-thing. For so many years. I was so determined. After working so hard at everything. All of a sudden. Nothing mattered. The zero impact I had on anything. It had a physical dimension. No project would ever matter. Nothing would last. I started too late. Every decision I made. Ever since I was very young. Had led me further from the path. I had failed in a very real and complete way. Everything I had ever done was an attempt to make up for this fact. Everything I had ever done was excusing my failure to meet the minimum standard. Set by myself. Set by everyone else. This hit me suddenly. I had to sit down. I was claustrophobic. There was no activity I could do that would make me forget. Every activity was only an attempt to make me forget. Nobody needed my opinion. My opinion only led them astray. My opinion only led me astray. The only thing I should do was nothing. I should never do anything. Ever again. Everything I bumped into put the world further out of orbit. What so many dying artists feel right before they perish. Forever. I realized. When these artists tell their loved ones to burn everything they have ever created. They did not find The Way. Their failure will only lead others astray. However. There is always the wicked hope. They did find The Way. However. They themselves never realized it. I faked my way through the rest of the presentation. I forced a smile. Nobody could tell. I was making fun of myself. Nobody could tell. I was making fun of the presentation, everyone in the room, and the universe itself. I started to wonder if everyone presented in this manner. If this was the key to a great presentation. Everyone ate it up. I crushed it. Several individuals had to visibly restrain themselves from providing a standing ovation. A standing ovation would have been inappropriate given the mundane subject matter. Several others were not so successful in restraining themselves. I blushed, attempting to give some of the credit to my team. They were "The real heroes today."

People who change the world never ask for permission. Psychopaths never ask for permission. Businessmen never ask for permission. Babies never ask for permission. Zarathustra never asked for permission. Zeus never asked for permission. Buddha never asked for permission. Jesus never asked for permission. Muhammed never asked for permission. God never asked for permission. Odin never asked for permission. Allah never asked for permission. Marilyn Monroe never asked for permission. Hitler never asked for permission. Rosa Parks never asked for permission. Champions never ask for permission. Cupid's arrow never asks for permission. Convincing lovers never ask for permission. Rapists never ask for permission. Murderers never ask for permission. Cancer never asks for permission. Disease never asks for permission. Sound never asks for permission. Death never asks for permission. The Unforeseen never asks for permission. The night never asks for permission. The day never asks for permission. The universe never asks for permission. You. You are the only one who has ever asked for permission. Ever. Why?

We haven't found a shorthand for these philosophical theories. We haven't found the shortcut. The limited number of actual moves that lay behind the elaborate, ornate moves. What doesn't move behind the elaborate illusion? What are the pillars? What is the smaller equation that unlocks the more elaborate working parts? Our passions? The universe? What is the shortcut, the summation, the three moves we can make every time in every situation? Why three? I have no idea. It's the first number I thought of.

But no. All this reduction. We should be working in the other direction. We should be multiplying into infinity. Never limiting. Always expanding. Never simplifying into maxims, dichotomies, and taxonomies. We should be exploding into an unconscious ability to do all things. Reduction is a safety net. A formula is a crutch. Everything you need, you should be able to access through your surroundings. Never written down. Never memorized. Always waiting to become. Everything else is weakness. He wrote.

Everything golden already occurred. It can only be golden if encapsulated within a memory. Even the bad. That golden existence. Warm, alive, passionate, but only accessed through the smell of damp pavement, an orange, scented candles, gazing in wonder at tempestuous skies. Sunbeams playing on the carpet where I lay. Mother is baking. Always eternities away. The division created by journeys never sought. Torn asunder from moments that might have been. Now so long ago. What was supposed to happen. Never did. Now so far from a gestured path. This path that was never obtainable. Flashes of European street visions. Old brick. Rich brown leather. Candlelight. Dusty volumes of books. There was magic. An orchestra's string section in the distance. Everything was grand. This was romance. Dark nights. Flickering lights. Damp grass under large oak trees. Meandering party-goers proclaiming it was too early for anything to end.

I remember a Wednesday. I was riding the bus back from work. I got off the bus to walk down a road. I had never been down this road before. I had passed it everyday. I don't know why I did this. Part of me wanted to make sure it wasn't a prop. It actually led somewhere. As far as I was willing to walk. The next bus didn't come for quite a while. I felt immensely foolish. But when I was back on the next bus, I still hadn't learned my lesson. I felt it overwhelmingly. Everything was rigged against me. They barely keep me alive. Life should be pleasant enough for me not to kill myself. Life should make me pissed enough to keep working at a breakneck pace. What am I pursuing? Why I am destined to be a master of none? Forever. Nobody wants me to achieve anything. But they also hate me when I fail. Lately, they have been pushing me towards total destruction. Forcefully. Heavy-handedly. What would happen if I let them be right about me? Fine. I won't amount to anything. I don't understand who this benefits. Another public-service announcement about the dangers of depression appeared on the television. Even this seems a bit heavy-handed. Maybe they are losing their touch? Who is behind this? All my ridiculous failed romantic pursuits. All my ridiculous failed everything. My superiors? The government? My friends and family? The higher-lifeforms that control everything? All my devices are bugged. My computer. My phone. My apartment. But why? What are they getting out of this? Capturing the human experience? A study conducted by some corporation? Wouldn't they want to capture the best of the human experience as well? It doesn't seem like it would be very difficult to provide me with a hint of that. Would it? Who would benefit from this ridiculous charade? I failed to generate plausible explanations. This played nicely into their hands. Regardless. It all seems highly predictable. Very mundane. I could almost predict when something was going to go wrong. Maybe that wasn't a special power of mine. Maybe things simply go wrong often. Surely this couldn't be worthwhile for anyone else.

I went to a pet store today. Or was it yesterday? I convinced myself that if I got a pet, I would feel better about everything. If I was responsible for another lifeform, I would have a new lease on life. It could trust me. It could depend on me. I looked into the eyes of every creature. I saw my own sadness. Something I did not need: the perpetual darkness of another being's soul haunting me every day. So I almost got one of the birds with clipped wings. Then I realized how heartbroken I'd be once the bird played silent witness to my shamefully depressing existence. The existence of his master of none. After the fall of his first, last, and only idol he would wander aimlessly through his remaining bird years. He would wander without hope and without purpose. He would become more and more like me. "I would just disappoint you." I told him this. I said it out loud. I'm not sure I meant to. I think the lady at the front counter heard me. She was hiding a smile. I walked out. Quickly. Red-faced.

When we die, we live everything over again in reverse and at the same speed. This is what that acid-dropping soliloquist told me on the bus. Or it was my own theory. I forget. We would play silent witness to the movie of our life. We would witness what our memory had purposefully distorted. We would be able to ask why. We would be able to witness what we got right. We would be able to witness what we got right but doubted. And then unnecessarily acted against ourselves. Perhaps we were right about nothing. This scenario is much more likely. Even more likely still, we wouldn't be able to view anything critically the second time around. We would forget everything just as easily. We arrive back at our birth. We start anew. We are forever trapped between the end-points of our existence. Forever oscillating between the two poles of our existence. Remembering nothing. However. This is only one way to think about time. Is there anything essential about living in a perceived forward facing manner? Is this mere perception through and throughout? Why employ this perception? If mere perception through and throughout, nothing will stand in relation to the perceived forwardness of now time and a mere reversal of this direction will not do. Reversing time would be reversing air. There was never anything there to begin with. Instead time is also a lava field: random moments of disconnected bubbles that wander to the surface and burst.

For now. Just maintain. Just maintain. Repeat.

I was back at the laundromat when a special news report disrupted every-thing calm in the world. Our President who was not my President erupted onto the screen. He ordered us to be especially alert of suspicious looking individuals in our area. He even made it easy for us to remember. There was a slogan: "If you see something say something." He didn't educate us on what we were supposed to see or what were supposed to say. It was already assumed that we were well educated on what the enemy looked like. I still had no idea. I didn't want to report anyone. But also everyone. Including the President. He was the most suspicious. If I reported him, they would lock me up. I quickly scanned the laundromat. I was alone. The laundromat was my universe. For now. Why should I ever leave? The world is at war outside.

I was waiting in line at the bank. I was struck by a realization. I had a relentlessly habitual belief of purposefulness. Whatever I happened to be doing was of the utmost importance. The justification for this motivation has yet to be corroborated. My approach was unfounded. I'll admit that much. However. It saved me from the devastating consequences that could have unfolded if didn't have access to this fantasy. My delusions of grandeur were a saving grace. As much as they damned me to total self-destruction. Oh well. Potential battles. I walked away from them. I adopted the opinion: they were below me. The erroneous heroic narrative. Destiny had me perpetually poised for greater things. Much greater than the petty rivalry laid out before me. This has saved me. This has wreaked havoc across the landscape of my existence. Maybe nothing is a bad thing. Maybe nothing is a good thing. Regardless. My surprisingly underwhelming success notwithstanding, at least I have my dignity. No I don't. But for an instant, it sounded like an industriously hopeful and heroic thing to say. If I believed it, it would be enough. If not, it wouldn't be. Unfortunately, I've started to see through my own illusions. They worked in the past. Like carrots in front of a horse. Soon, I will have to find a shitload of carrots. I need to go grocery shopping. I'll do that on Saturday. Maybe I will start eating better too. Like I did in the past. Probably not.

In this dimension the key is making it appear that you are normal to everyone while being completely abnormal: attempt to get along with as many people as possible but also don't have feelings for anyone or for anything. Everything will hurt you. You will hurt everyone. No matter what you do. In this dimension, you are beholden to no one and to nothing, including yourself. Especially yourself. Identity is a trap. Narrative is a trap. Everything is a trap. If you remember this, you will survive this very shitty, ass-backwards, confusing dimension. Admittedly, it is a very poorly constructed one. But you simply need to survive it. Simply survive.

I will be cursed with old age. Having said that, I will die too soon. Having said that, I will be cursed with old age. Etc. It will probably be neither.

Or both. Or one or the other. When I am cursed with old age (and right before I completely lose my mind), I will be able to look back upon all the worries I worried about and chuckle at their pointlessness. I don't think I'd laugh. I'd definitely chuckle. Maybe I'd smirk. I don't think I'd smirk. Smirking isn't becoming of anyone. It depends on who is watching me while I am I looking back upon all the worries I worried about. I wouldn't laugh. I wouldn't be that surprised at the pointlessness of my worries. I'm already writing about how pointless they are. It would be a chuckle. Or a smile with the shake of my head. If I were in the ideal setting for this to take place (sunny Italian piazza sipping espresso or wine if it's later in the day), some inquisitive young scholar (very sharply dressed with perfect skin) at the peak of their glorious golden youth and summer holiday away from the cares of a very prestigious university that I would have never been able to afford would ask me what made me chuckle (or smile knowingly with a shake of my head). I would smile. Wisely. Looking off into the distance I'd answer, "Don't worry about it. You fucking idiot."

I woke up in a panic. I was wrong about something. The panic subsided when I remembered who I was: someone who nobody depended on getting anything right. I had never been published. I had nothing at stake in the world of the living. Regardless. It was unnerving. Perhaps I've been wrong about my theories on society. But for all the right reasons. Society runs on complete pointlessness. All the idiots I blame for wasting our time are allowing us to live in a forgetful illusion. The illusion is all there is. The illusion is all there ever will be. All the idiots I blame for holding back the progress of humankind are actually keeping this whole thing going. Don't give them too much credit. They are entirely interchangeable. If not for them. Someone else. There is no such thing as progress. We who work to reveal the illusion are at fault. We who believe there is something other than the illusion are at fault. Myself included. Should I stop? It doesn't matter either way. It's impossible to defeat the illusions. They are too powerful. They are too seductive. Nobody wants to defeat them anyway. Not even myself. I tell myself I do. But I haven't yet. So I don't. The person who attempts to reveal illusions only provides more illusions.

Talk to someone. Tell them something you would never tell anyone. Do it right now.

When I finally did achieve success it felt hollow. I think back to the past. I had been applying to an excessive number of graduate schools. I received an acceptance letter. It wasn't the worst option. But by that point I understood the arbitrary nature of success and failure. Now I was being told I had won a prize. I envisioned the epitaph heroically engraved on my tombstone: "He came. He saw. He was mildly disappointed." I couldn't even be disappointed fully. I had to experience disappointment halfway as well. Success came with asterisks, fine print, and disclaimers. Awards and certifications arrived long past necessity, helpfulness, or thankfulness. Awards and certifications served as poor markers and arrant buoys on unnecessarily turbulent seas. If I hadn't been steering the ship, I would have been a cloud. I would have been a cloud laughing at everything below me. Someone was sparing no expense to cast me in this ridiculously grotesque performance. I'll never know if I figured out who it was. I'll never know why they needed me to entertain them—to be their source of pitiful laughter. This force abhors its victim's sense of self-respect. While others are let to roam free, ridiculously proclaiming their immortal god-like nature, this must not be tolerated from me. I must be punished. I am not told what my crime is. I must be punished because I am me. Others must be celebrated because they are they. Those running the show must remain hidden in plain sight. This is the way.

Modernity is merely the anxiety produced by the knowledge that humanity has missed the boat.

A fly made several attempts to crawl into my miserable apartment through a crack in the window. "Don't. It's worse in here." Even the fly thought it knew better than me. It didn't matter. It couldn't get through. It gave up. I'm sure there is something significant about this interaction. I can't think of anything. No really, I'm not sure why I even mentioned it. It's as pointless as everything else I've mentioned. Perhaps more so. Definitely more so. I'd erase it, but if I started to erase every pointless thing I've ever said or done, blank pages are all that would remain. Why start now?

I've witnessed insanity. But one does not become insane. It doesn't occur as it is typically depicted. No surprise there. It's not the individual who becomes insane. Instead, the outer world itself starts failing—not you. Insanity is not losing yourself in an illusion. Insanity is the complete loss of illusion altogether. Insanity is seeing reality for what it is. Completely. Without lies and illusions, we have no reason to live. Our lives are lies. Insanity is not a mental downgrade. This misconception is highly misleading. Insanity occurs when you have outsmarted the outer world and have outdistanced the intelligence of the outer world and the future it has planned out for you. That is what insanity is. When you are insane, the simulation has fallen a step behind you. You have seen everything for what it actually is. The problem: civilization, humanity, technology, logic, etc. have no means of accommodating your mental state. They have no way of translating the multiplicity. And so, nothing happens. What society doesn't understand they discard, fear, and shun. What makes you insane is not the fact that you are insane, but that everyone thinks you are, when you are really the only one who is seeing everything for how it actually is. Insanity is something that is done to you. Insanity is an external force that acts on you. Nobody can share what you are seeing. Madness. Self-perpetuating. In-communicably self-enhancing with no chance at all of the necessary break through. I don't know how I was able to pull out of the experience: the experience of insanity happening upon me. I believe I told myself to keep going. I believe I told myself that if I made it out, I would better off because of this knowledge. I don't know how I was able to remember what happened. It came back to me as I was typing. I might have even managed some semblance of verisimilitude in depicting the situation here. But at the time I had to lie to myself in order to avoid going insane. Even at the time I hardly believed myself. Some part of me did. Some part of me still wants to be part of this dimension. I have no idea why. I really don't like it here. It's not so bad when I'm drunk, stoned, getting laid, eating, showering, sleeping, accomplishing something, travelling, playing a game, or joking around. But otherwise. Fuck it.

It was my non-lover's birthday. I never believed in pre-mandated celebrations. If an individual was living a semi-decent life, they wouldn't need to be reminded of one of the most traumatic events in their existence in order to ensure their happiness one day out of the year. However. Lately, my sleep was poor to nonexistent. My thoughts raced. My paranoia grew more ridiculous. Or I was becoming more aware of my surroundings. I suspected my non-lover was somehow behind all this. Not too long ago, I woke up in the middle of the night (very early in the morning) at her place. I wasn't sure why I woke up. Aided by the lite semi-dream state I was in, I recalled a few moments back. She had been poking me. I looked over. She was fake sleeping. Or was she actually asleep? An impossible situation. So I was going to bake her a birthday cake as an act of resistance: even though she was slowly driving me insane, I could still function as a regular human. Her attempts were failing. I was adapting to my new insanity. However. In order to bake the cake, I needed to clean my kitchen. This would require me to purchase supplies. Like soap. I also needed to purchase a pan to bake the cake. I needed cake supplies. I would have to go to the store. But first I needed to write all this down. So I looked for a pen and paper. I could not find either in my shitty apartment. I knocked on my neighbor's door. A child answered. I asked if their parent's where home. They shrugged and motioned for me to come inside. I didn't know what that meant. I said "Hello" loudly. To nobody in particular. Obviously, I did not remember my neighbor's names. I got a sinking feeling. The child was home alone. Watching TV. I quickly asked if there was a pen and paper around, not expecting a reply, as I scanned the room looking to borrow something to write on and leave immediately. Too late. The front door started to open. In walked the neighbors. They were visibly upset to see me. Understandably so. My gut reaction was to start apologizing profusely. I attempted an inaudible explanation of the impossible situation that transpired. It went poorly. It was answered by expletives. Loud expletives. They were motioning me toward the door. I don't believe I will be welcome over there again. Needless to say, I returned to my apartment with no writing capabilities. I went to the store regardless. I barely had enough money to pay for everything. I returned home and cleaned the kitchen. I realized I had forgotten several essential ingredients. It was too late to go back to the store. I crawled into bed and attempted to pretend the day away. My non-lover came over. She was very upset with me. She assumed I forgot her birthday.

The constant self-policing. Checking-in to evaluate my social acceptability. Nauseating self-discipline. But I doubted equally: if censoring myself had ever helped me achieve anything and my ability to have ever censored myself. Oh well. All the institutions. All the morally corrective forces. Built to convince me of their disciplinary merits. I played their game (or did I?). I did what I was told (or did I?). I followed their rules (or did I?). The results were indistinguishable. I would be much better off if I didn't follow the rules. I followed their rules, but they could tell I didn't believe in their rules. It's a far greater crime to follow their rules without believing in them. I followed the rules, but I didn't do it with a smile. Others completely discarded the rules. They did it with a smile. They still believed in the rules. They just chose not to follow them. They were rewarded. But I was not them. They were they. They could get away with it because they always had. I could not get away with it because I never had. I had a foot in both streams. Blindly flailing at my adversaries. Fighting with one hand behind my back. This is what they hated most. They want to love you. They want you to be their enemy, so they can love to hate you. Now they can convert you. Anything in-between simply isn't profitable. Silence, certain forms of humor, and disinterest will not be tolerated.

I got stoned later that night. I realized I was doing most of my living elsewhere. I was living an entirely different life in this daydreamed elsewhere. I was spending too much time in a simultaneous multiverse. The gap was impossible. I can't live with each universe so far apart from me. Like a mirror they show me where I am—ultimately apart from them. I can only see them. I cannot be them. I cannot be myself. One particular universe found me a well known and respected individual amongst other talented and genuine individuals. My house was brick and rich leather. There were whole afternoons devoted to fun. There were rigorous and intellectually stimulating creative projects. There were no deadlines. There was romance in everything. There were smiling faces. Always understanding. Throughout everything. There was understanding.

Where you are is the place you are. Until you are no longer in that place. Then you are no longer there. This thought pattern became necessary. Lately, my mind was producing especially disturbing thoughts to obsessively panic about. These thoughts were brought on by the simulated nature of my universe, the fact that nothing changed regardless of what I did, the impossibility of pure happiness or advancement, etc. Therefore, I strongly considered the possibility that my body was stuck in a coma elsewhere. Realizing this at once. Fully. It was becoming too much. What was the way out? Through death? Through pure insanity? Next time I feel the voiceless voices, do I let them take me? The present I'm living in now could be an illusory state of reality. As I am stuck in this dream state, every remedy to prevent the panic-attack of a complete existential crisis from pulling me into the depths and keeping me down there, was actually preventing me from aligning myself back with my body in the coma. Every survival instinct and every action previously assumed to be "good" for me was only taking me further down an illusory path away from myself. With every step forward, I was moving further away. Further away from being able to wake up. Ever. As I became more involved with this life, I became less interested in searching for the truth. And I would no longer believe the truth if I discovered it. Everything I knew and loved in this life was an illusion constructed by my brain to withstand the trauma of being trapped in a coma. Everything that kept me in this life was pushing me downward into deeper levels of the simulation, of the dream state, etc. I was moving further underwater. The lake had frozen over. However. Perhaps I was self-generating this grand illusion of reality for other reasons. For example, my body could be someplace less hopeful than in a hospital bed. I could be buried alive in a coffin. I could be in a straight jacket unjustly locked in a padded room. But that wasn't the worst part. Although highly improbably, perhaps I found a way to fight back to my body. For example, if I spent an eternity in this purgatory-reality building a spaceship to fly through a black hole and back to my body in a coma. Or if I broke the spell by becoming the world's smartest scientist/philosopher and discovered I was a brain in a vat, or that we live in a virtual reality world. Or I time traveled back to the right time where my body was in a coma, in the coffin, or in the straight jacket, and some how I broke free. However. Even if I woke up in what I thought was my "proper" body and lived on, there would be no way to tell if I wasn't merely in another state of pure illusion. My real body could still be in another dormant state somewhere else. From that point on, it would always only feel as if I could peel back another layer to reach reality. Where you are is the place you are. Until you are no longer in that place. Then you are no longer there.

I was in the past now. Standing in line at the bank. Wasting my valuable lunchtime. I was reminded of the time I traveled to Europe. I couldn't figure out the train system. Looking back, it was fairly simple. I was flustered in the moment. It's a good thing we don't have to report our most idiotic moments. It's a good thing we've found ways to cover up our most idiotic moments that are witnessed publicly. Otherwise, we would all be sent back to elementary school or declared criminally insane. A beautiful Dutch girl saw me struggling and offered to help. I asked her if she spoke English in Dutch. It was one of the only two phrases I learned. And badly. She did. We struck up a nice conversation. She spent the afternoon guiding me around. We probably would have fallen in love. As in a movie. Of course she had a boyfriend. She was meeting him. For literary purposes, if we pretend she didn't have a boyfriend, and we fell in movie-love, I would have had my own stupidity to thank for our initial meeting. Is our own misguided stupidity a saving grace? Does stupidity have evolutionary benefits? Confidence often plays a major role in determining whether or not an individual can successfully complete a task. Confidence often takes a radical amount of stupidity. Stupidity has radically beneficial properties in religion and politics as well. Here, idiotic fearmongering demagogues play on stupidity to garner support from the idiotic masses. Our President bypassed all intellectual appeals to reason on his way to winning the election. I've been overlooking stupidity as the answer to all my problems.

If falling asleep is a dress rehearsal for death, I will be very bad at dying. Right before bed there is still so much left to do. I have accomplished nothing in life.

I'm being written out of my own story. I'm running out of options. I've always been running out of options. Life is the process of running out of options. At crucial moments the wrong thing happened. I know. This is the wrong way to think. Regardless, everything feels wrong. It's suppose to. If these higher-Beings can keep me in a constant state of mild disappointment, my achievement striving blindness will solve their puzzle. I am making all the wrong decisions on purpose. Whenever I have taken a stand, I should have waited it out. I should have done nothing. Whenever I ran, I should have stayed. Whenever I stayed, I stayed far too long. I'm wrong for this world. How alone can someone be? I knew the answer. Always waiting for life to happen. Perpetually unbalanced. All this to solve their problem. I've never found a cause, a belief, a religion, a politics, a romance, a team, a home. I hear the voice of a disapproving elder: "You should feel fortunate. Think about the poor children in (insert miserably unfortunate corner of the world here)." This never does anything for me. The misery of others does not console me. What can I trust? It becomes difficult to distinguish the point when it all slipped away. Who could I ever trust? Luckily, I am the only person left whom I can fully untrust. However, this doesn't seem to be a reason to celebrate.

If I think all the thoughts there are to think, it's not improbable that one of them will push me into another dimension. However. If I think all the thoughts there are to think, it's still highly unlikely she will ever love me.

I'm back in the past now. For no apparent reason, I peered into my mediocre cup of coffee. I was at work. This reminded me. The other night, another typical, paranoid, philosophical-ish thought had crept into my mind while drunk, stoned, and watching an educational documentary. The DNA written in our genetic code isn't random. The DNA written in our genetic code is the conscious planning of the DNA itself. We aren't controlled by higher-alien Beings from in outer space. We are controlled by small microscopic conscious Beings. They are so small we deny their agency. But how can we consider them small? They make up everything. We are not an accidental mutation. We serve a purpose for the DNA-gods. What is their purpose for me? To keep on procreating? When will they have the answer they are looking for? When will they have their final creation? No. They don't think in those terms. They don't think at all. They just create. That is what makes them the higher-lifeform. They don't ask questions. How would we ever usurp an entity that never questions? How would we ever usurp an entity that produces whatever it wants without hesitation? Cloning? Changing the structure ourselves? This is merely another way for them to tighten their grip. Merely another way for them to produce the results they desire through us. Perhaps mentally? We must travel outside all logic, all tradition, and listen to everything that our DNA has in common with everything else. If we can accomplish this, we will instantly gain the story/memory of everything and move with it at all times in every thought. In every action. There was nothing in my cup, but more mediocre coffee. Oh well.

I smiled. Apparently I made an optimistic note to myself. Last night. Before I passed out. I was drinking whiskey: "Of whiskey, if I could live my life three glasses deep, I could conquer the world in a week." I should be a motivational speaker. Or an interior decorator. I came downstairs to a couch that was miraculously balanced upside-down on its thinnest part. To this day I have no explanation as to how or why this occurred. It brought the room together nicely.

My reality started to make less sense. My dreams became more vivid. This cosmic joke was cliché. The laughing audience, the future. Is everyone around me capable of being in on the joke? More likely, figments of my imagination. Eventually, I can discern my dreams as dreams. Perhaps I will be able to discern waking life as a dream. In due time. Waking life is simply the longest dream yet. No. I am not listening. Cause and effect has confused. I've put too much importance on this waking life. Cause and effect is addictive. It trains and physically forms the brain. Every piece of information is used to make sense of my narrative. But I have not lived my whole life. Perhaps all we can conclude is this: the authority of this waking life rests on obtaining the highest degree of our investment in its perception. We tread on unstable ground.

My friends who were not my friends were back in town. I did not want to see them. I also desperately needed to leave the apartment. Maybe if I got really drunk and ignored their personalities, I could convince myself they were my buddies from back home. Before the war. Or during another war. If there were any wars. I proceeded to down very cheap liquor. It stung but it worked. I started believing this was a good idea. I showed up to meet them. Perhaps I was overly enthusiastic. Perhaps it was lunch time. They gave me strange looks. They were mildly interesting to me. I didn't order food. I ordered more drinks. They looked very concerned. They asked me a lot of questions about my career path. About my goals in life. I thought it was a hoot. They were not amused. Lunch took a sharp turn. This was an intervention. I attempted to explain. I wasn't an alcoholic. I drank to make them interesting. However. I thought better of it. I might need a job someday. Although I would hate working for them. Or anywhere adjacent to their universe. Regardless. I attempted to test the waters during the intervention. I was drunk enough to act against my own free-will, "Well, if any of you high-level business managers would hire me, maybe that could help me out of my situation here?" Their response was unanimous: "We wouldn't hire you. You're a drunk."

I was at the grocery store. I was waiting in line. I forget if this was last Monday or last Thursday. It was either daytime or nighttime. I was thinking about something important. I remember thinking it was important at the time. Now, I have no idea what I was thinking about. I looked up. I read an employee's nametag. It said Darwin. I thought: our thoughts could be subject to evolutionary-type process. So could our narratives. What are the factors that determine which narratives survive from generation to generation? From person to person? From day to day within ourselves? The narratives that multiply fastest? The narratives that are most complete/strongest? The ones that are more appealing to the most people? The ones that are able to motivate? Regardless of direction? The common reference point drags everything down with it. We would only be as good as the most common thinkers. Every thought you've ever had. Every thought I've ever had. We are having an impact. Are we? Are your idiot thoughts holding back all of humanity? Are my idiot thoughts holding back all of humanity? Harmful mutations indistinguishable from helpful changes. The ability to distinguish is dependent on the evolution of thoughts. As I am writing.

We don't want it to be true. But we suspect that the closest we get to immortality is having our likeness preserved by whatever discourse of fame we bet will survive in perpetuity.

Looking out the window. I reflect on the moment. The first moment. My one chance. It is part of every moment. Before and after. You already know the outcome. Perhaps I always already did too. It is now every suspicion. Hesitation. Doubt. The events stream in now unabated. The opinions have been formed. Now it's never the event itself. It is as well. The memory. Is it mine anymore? A stadium of people. Expectations. How did it happen? My body went numb. What I wasn't expecting. A routine moment. This has never happened before. It will never happen again. I never had the chance. That is how things end. That is how reoccurring dreams begin.

These dreams. Don't worry, there will be another season next year. I wake up. It isn't true. These dreams. Don't worry, she'll come back to you. I wake up. It isn't true. These dreams. Don't worry, you'll become what you are supposed to become. I wake up. It isn't true. Projected forward and backward into my life. All eras now permeated with suspiciously inconsistent failures. I am provided with poor excuses for enemies and rivals. I reject them all. A life half lived.

Imagine how smart I'd be if I could simply recall what I already know. But I can't. I'm not even as smart as myself.

My lover who was not my lover wanted us to have dinner with another couple. She went to school with them. When she got me drunk a few nights ago she quickly mentioned that she very briefly dated the male aspect of the couple. They dated but this was a very long time ago before he met the female aspect of the couple. I couldn't care any less. But I wanted to see if he might take my non-lover back. However. She confused my complete indifference for emotional maturity and a sign that our relationship was even more stable than she originally thought. I did not realize this until much later. Otherwise I would have acted very jealous at dinner. Instead, I inwardly mocked them. It became abundantly clear that the couple had invested a lot of time overthinking this dinner. My non-lover had given it a great deal of thought as well. But nobody was as invested in this dinner as her ex-lover. Much to the visible chagrin of his current wife, he was still madly in love with my non-lover. His true affections surfaced in the attention to detail he showed her in conversation, the all-too-eager offering of napkins and utensils, the pointlessly old-fashioned trope of standing beside his chair whenever she wasn't seated, etc. His current wife was outwardly lovely. She was a vision. If he (and perhaps a long succession of individuals in her life) paid more attention to her, she probably wouldn't be annoying. She spent most of the dinner relentlessly vying for scraps of importance. It's possible that she was as artificial as he was. She fished for compliments. Asking about my non-lover's more modest jewelry so that my non-lover would in turn complement her gaudy oversized string of pearls. The whole dinner I was wondering how to properly propose a couple's swap. Just for the night. The table was void of many things.

It was not void of propriety. There was an abundance. There was a lot of confusingly pleasant passive-aggressive jousting from the members of the table who had something at stake. Namely everyone but myself, who was merely a spectator at the wonderful bloodsport of true love. It was not long before the ex-lover was talking about what he did for a living. My mind purposefully avoided taking in any of the information he was providing. He made a lot of money screwing over people who didn't know any better and deserved it least. He failed to provided any essential benefits for society, but he earned the respect of nearly everyone in society including every female at our table. My mind wandered, as I smiled and nodded vigorously. He was hardly looking at me anyway. He was honing in on my non-lover. Thank goodness. Self-promotion is what we turn to when we have nothing to do. It is the remainder, the carry-over, the residual. Perhaps it represents our economy. When there is no sense to be made, when all our purposeful reasoning is exhausted, we surrender and relegate everything to "the economy" to sort out. This is merely another way of saying: "We desire an unknown inefficiency to decide for us." It is the unconscious that we are giving ourselves over to. The necessary forgetting that must take place. The period at the end of the sentence. The grounding that allows everything else to pivot forward. The sacrifice that must leave itself behind to mark time. The event. The memorial. "What do you do?" Everyone was looking at me. "Nothing." This was apparently too abrupt. It was not going to suffice for a reasonable answer. This is what I surmised after the well-to-do couple across the table assumed I was joking. I caught a vicious stare from my non-lover out of the corner of my eye. I started to smile, playing it off as a joke, "...meaning, that I'm somewhat of a master of none at the moment, but I've got my hand in a lot pots right now. I'm waiting for the right market conditions. You understand?" I gestured at the ex-lover, who, not wanting to look like a simpleton nodded in agreement. He had no idea how to read me. I was both incredibly vague and incredibly confident. Not because I was better than him, but because I simply didn't care about anything he cared about. I was fine with leaving things at that. My non-lover stepped in. "He's very well educated." The couple across the table nodded knowningly. They did not know what to do with this additional information. There was awkward silence. I loved it. I wasn't going to say anything. The ex-lover's wife broke the silence by excusing herself to use the restroom. As she stood up, her husband remaind seated. I mockingly stood up to remind him. He embarrassingly saw the error of his ways. He shot out of his chair like a bolt of lightening. He face was beet red.

It was either last Tuesday or Friday. I was at the bus stop. I devised a method. To begin with, the individual admits that everything they've ever told themselves is merely a lie to make themselves feel better about every bad situation they've ever been in and every bad decision they've ever made. From this point forward, the individual attempts to move away from this claim. The individual can disprove this claim by providing evidence that this claim is unnecessarily overbearing. Furthermore, (hopefully) the individual's strengths and good decisions come rushing in to remind them that at one point the individual had strengths and made good decisions. They should be copied for future use. But if past strengths and good decisions do not apply to the situation under evaluation, they should be dismissed for the remainder of the exercise and not used as a crutch. When evaluating this evidence, the individual is given the opportunity to envision the situation and determine if, given the same circumstances, they would have repeated their actions. At the very least, once the individual has become comfortable with these first steps, this initial process can slowly reveal how one could have handled the situation differently. Eventually, if it turns out they could have improved the situation, their initial perception can be broken down: they can observe their holistically flawed approach. With even more practice, the individual can observe a thoroughly flawed aspect of their entire Being. This method can only commence if the individual is willing to admit at the outset that everything they have ever told themselves is a lie to make themselves feel better. If this is your grounding point (if at least from time to time), you will no longer perpetually remain unwittingly self-righteous. You will no longer remain eternally confused as to why most people don't like you. I wish someone had given me this advice when I was a functioning member of society.

I had a dream last month. I was an artist. Tonight was my night. Opening night. Big city gallery exhibition. My first introduction to the big time. To this scene. To this city. There were rumors. Great anticipation. Many years built up to this. I was confident in the work. The time came. Everything went according to plan. I was thrilled. This was the best night of my life. I was introduced to everyone. To the most formidable critic. She only wrote importance. A ridiculously long cigarette filter. It matched her ridiculously long high heels. Puffs of smoke and a heavily caked leather face mumbled ice words. "We liked your earlier work better." I couldn't tell if she was joking. She had never told a joke in her life. "But you haven't seen my earlier work." The pointy leather cake responded. "Yes, we liked you better that way." I woke up. It was just a dream. I was still pissed. It was too familiar. It ruined my weekend.

I can't remember. What cavernous recess of my brain was I drawing from? The acidhead's ramblings on the bus? A scientific paper? A dream? I could simply be thinking it now. In our descriptions of the universe, we assume we are the center. Other planets are certain light-years away from us. This implies that they are occurring in the past in relation to us. Time is distance. Time is personal. This will be observed later. But why should we be occurring in the present? Why should we be in the center of time/distance? Other planets harbor time/distance-keeping lifeforms. They are projecting their time/distance measurement outward. Why shouldn't we use their perception/projection of time/distance? We don't even attempt to guess what their perception/projection of time/distance would be. We are thinking in linear time/distance when we project outwards into time/distances away from us. There is no center to the universe. There is no central zero point from which time/distance starts or stops. There is no one view that perceives/experiences time/distance from the zero point, from the center. Should/n't there be? We model off the assumption that we are the center of the universe. We are modeling ourselves after the center of the universe. We align our time(distance)line with the time(distance)line of the center of the universe. But there is no time(distance) line. Time/distance is a false indicator used to distract us. Distract us from what? Who benefits from us being distracted by concerns over time/distance? This is the wrong question. Is it? Oh well. It is madness to give up. Or was it madness to have begun in the first place?

A loud explosion outside my apartment. My apartment shook. Emergency sirens. People screamed. This was it. The war was here. I ran to the window. The broken tailpiece of an aircraft was in the middle of the street. It crushed a car. A fire started. It was beautifully silhouetted by the night. The whole scene was a contemporary art exhibit. Out my window. But free admission. Emergency vehicles were arriving. I rushed outside. Everything started to move in slow motion. Now I saw the rest of the plane. A commercial airliner. Further down the street. It had plowed into another apartment building. Emergency crews were rescuing people trapped inside. Some of them wouldn't survive. I'm sure most of the people on the plane hadn't survived. My first instinct was to help. I'm not sure what I was going to do. I stood dumbly. Until I realized they were blocking off the area from onlookers. I asked a fellow onlooker, "Does this mean the war has started?" The onlooker wasn't necessarily responding to my question. They remained staring straight ahead. The distant look in their eyes. They made up their mind up a long time ago about what happened tonight. "Them terrorists did this."

I still make predictions. I still move heaven and earth to prove I'm right. I still think I've found truth. I'm still a human. Living among humans. I always already know this way is wrong. But I could be wrong. At least these ways aren't as present in my art. Maybe they are. Perhaps my art is the training ground for minimizing these ways throughout the rest of my life. Follow your art?

I was waiting for the bus again. I had another strange thought. As stated previously. We are wrong. Babies are smarter than we have ever imagined. Taking this further. They are in charge of everything. Their minds free from the pollution of silly ambitions, trite rivalries, and hackneyed narrative expectations. They have super mind powers that control the cosmos. Our adult minds are full of pointless distractions. We have no way to perceive that babies are telepathically in charge of everything. We devolve over the course of our lives and as a species. We can never remember. At one point, we had incredible powers. Our minds have become fixated on pointless distractions. Modern adults can never be trusted with such powers. We would merely subject these powers to our fanciful whims. This would be detrimental to everything. We don't know what we want. We only know what we want in relation to what we can't have. So we have no idea if we actually want it. Upon receiving it, we are only fulfilling an expectation. We confuse expectation with desire. We confuse desire with self. Babies are in charge of everything. As it should be.

Tell someone the truth about something you have lied about.

I was beginning to wonder whether I enjoyed cigarettes as much as I enjoyed sitting outside by myself. I stopped smoking cigarettes. Now I sit outside and do nothing. I often have nothing to think about during social interactions. During these moments I try to determine the strangest thing I could do. Standing in the checkout line in the grocery store I've thought about jumping on top of the conveyor belt. I would stand motionless and allow the conveyor belt to take me all the way to the cashier. Upon arrival I would promptly dismount and step back in line. When meeting the incredibly forgettable wife of someone incredibly forgettable at an incredibly forgettable party, I've thought about asking her to marry me on the spot. During a stuffy conference I've thought about interrupting the presenter in order to publicly denounce the act of sitting. Following this denunciation, I would move on to accuse the person sitting next to me of leaving the water running at their house. I wonder if instead of thinking these thoughts, I were able to think about the speed of light, brain surgery, solving world hunger, etc. then maybe I would be some kind of genius famous person. A genius famous person who loudly orders lobster cream pie at a family restaurant and then proceeds to lie naked on the floor and play dead for several hours.

If god did exist, it would hate the majority of the people who believe in it. God loves talent. The kind of talent that is fought for. The kind of talent that is achieved without making excuses. God favors this above all. Above all other people, god appreciates those who are genuinely attempting to understand themselves and their world—those who question everything but who are not debilitated by this questioning. But god does not exist. Too bad. I could get on board with this version of god. Oh well.

I was drunk on an airplane. I attempted to write some poetry: "I sat with my gin and tonic. She walked across the room. My eyes followed. She turned. I looked away. She asked me. I fell off my chair. This happened hours ago. I'm still here on the floor."

I was back at the diner. I was waiting for coffee. I got the idea to come back here. I don't know from where. I thought outside. Outside of imagining some alien lifeform in outer space controlling everything. Outside of imagining our DNA as a higher-power. Instead. Our ideas are the higher-lifeform. They are in charge. They comfort us and take care of us. We comfort babies when they are anxious. They don't know. Religion, Science, and Philosophy comfort us when we are anxious. We don't know. These ideals. These theories. Narratives. These self-made gods. They control and comfort us. We give them power. Kings, presidents, militaries, and governments. They align themselves with this power. They want to disappear behind this power.

My mind wandered to the past. How I found myself in this position. The alien bitch acting as my superior. Our President who was not my President's royal decree: every individual is required to have letters of recommendation from their superiors if they desire advancement. This insured subordination. It preserved the hierarchy. I asked each of my superiors politely. I gave them plenty of notice. The alien scheduled a meeting with me. She told me I was the most disorganized individual to ever ask her for a letter of recommendation. I told her I would ask someone else to write the letter. She threw a fit. Her grip was growing weaker. She was losing her ability to negatively affect my life. She took the matter directly to the superior superior to reprimand my brash actions. I still had to meet the application deadline. I met with the superior superior. Without any detailed knowledge of the situation the superior superior (who I suspected was also an alien) threatened to fire me immediately without any recommendations. He had "Just about had it with me." I had no idea. I hardly interacted with him. He said this was yet another reckless outburst in a long line of reckless outbursts. I think he had me confused with someone else. Or he was rehearsing lines for a theatrical performance. It's obvious now: they were both from another planet. They were hell-bent on holding back humanity. I pretended to apologize profusely. Aliens do not understand sarcasm. He wasn't finished. He provided a lecture on how to treat people. He thought I was much younger than I was. I'm not sure who he was talking to. He wasn't talking to me. The speech was aimed at someone else. It was very out of place. It was prerecorded and played at the wrong time. I didn't respond. There was nothing to respond to. I had no emotional attachment to anything that was going on. I needed to submit letters of recommendation by a deadline. In the end, I never got hired. The aliens won.

Someone called me. Nobody I knew. They asked me to be a participant in a study they were conducting. I told them I was mentally unstable. They asked me if I was lying. I told them I didn't know. There was a long pause. They told me I'd make a perfect candidate. I hung up. Theirs was a lost cause. Put a cross section of citizens in a room. Let them serve as a focus group and plan for the future based on the results. This has failed us. Put politicians in a room. Have them draft policies to make our world a better place. This has failed us. Put a hiring committee in a room. Have them select the best candidates for a very important position. This has failed us. Put corporate executives and the heads of every major bank in a room. Have them fix the global economy and eliminate poverty. This has failed us. Put the world's religious leaders in a room. Have them stop their all-knowing-gods from making us commit the most heinous acts against each other. This has failed us. We must be designing rooms wrong.

Cleaning up my filthy apartment. I don't know why. Regardless. It will always look filthy. Constantly attempting to reduce the filth. Cutting away. Working towards singularity. One theory. Every unification creates its own un-unification. For its future unification. We need to shortcut the process beforehand. We need to construct a dis-unification unifier that takes apart the original theory so fast and puts it back together that when the process is complete, all the permutations have occurred, and we will have the final product. This might defeat the purpose of theory construction. Perhaps theory construction is supposed to be a distraction. There are never any true answers. Further evidence that we are merely living in a game-like simulation. Perhaps there are other reasons for theory construction that we do not understand? This is just the kind of question one would ask to distract someone else from the fact that we are in a game-like simulation. And so on ad infinitum.

Standing proudly. A complete imbecile. Loudly shout your stupidity. Hear the echoed refrain. And—with grace—move to the side. I stared out the window. I remember. I wanted to go to the desert to turn thirty. I had told myself this was the only place to turn thirty. What was I going to have been. When was I suppose to me. At this age. At the next. To go to the place that won't give you the answer. The place to face the question. Could you hear if you tried. To go to the place that is the question. Look at the calendar. There are years you won't see. You haven't even begun to become.

A million years and yesterday. Her face.

The story of my life. I was thinking within the terms of the television advertisement blaring at me. I couldn't sleep. Again. Again. I can only put myself within a narrative we both already know. My motives are so benign. I wonder why I haven't been stoned to death by my family and friends. I am a broken record. Repeat. Repeat. I am tired of my own narrative. I'm supposed to be the most interested. I've been forced to be interested. Forced for reasons of professionalization. For self-preservation. To get ahead in life. For a while, constant fear and paranoia kept me invested. But I learned. Those were merely survival instincts. They kick-in when our lives' have become so boring and depressing that there is nothing else to keep us interested. I don't care anymore. Forced interest in my life doesn't make me very interested. I've experienced too many things to believe my life matters in a grand scheme. Or that there is a grand scheme. We see nothing of anything that matters to something we are remotely interested in. I will begin the story of my life when the story is worth telling.

The following is a story I wrote many nights ago. In the past. After I had been out all night drinking. I think I stole it from an ancient Chinese proverb. "Once there was a stork who stood waiting patiently for a fish. A circling hawk watched the stork from above. The hawk couldn't figure out why the stork was standing so still. The hawk flew down and landed on a nearby branch. He asked the stork, 'Why are you standing so still?' The stork replied, 'I'm hunting.' The hawk laughed and said mockingly, 'I don't see how you are going to catch anything that way.' 'Patience has its rewards,' replied the stork. In a couple of minutes, a fish swam by the stork who jabbed quickly and caught it. The hawk said, 'Sure, you caught a fish, but it took you forever. Watch me, I will show you how to hunt efficiently.' The hawk flew high into the sky. Spotting a sparrow far below him, the hawk began his fast descending attack. A plane was flying by and the hawk was sucked into its powerful engine and died. The engine blew up. The plan crashed. Killing the stork below."

Organizing. That will keep me moving. That will make the motion forward. I started with my room. Next. My desk, notes, files, and folders were put in order. To ready me for future chaos. I found a pen and paper that would have helped me at some point. I forget why now. My mind wandered. I listened to recommended music. I hadn't had time to listen to it. I hadn't had time to get over so much. Even last week's embarrassingly pathetic shenanigans when I went out after raiding my own liquor cabinet. I can never let anything go. That's not true. See? Even that. I was bad at prioritizing, contextualizing, and efficiently dealing with mistakes. Worse than anyone else? Perhaps not. This awareness of my inability made it worse. I could never escape. Overthinking. But I could build monuments. I look back on these monuments. Written or otherwise. I am surprised. I hate and love them in ways. I am always completely oblivious to. Is this the way we live? How do we ever have confidence? These monuments provide an ever-renewing possibility to cringe. They are void of poetry. They are too poetic for their own good. That said. Monument building is better than killing oneself.

Cringe-making angst. Organizing helped distract. I always took issue with those who railed against distraction. The attempt to teach the other into a self un-made reality. Distraction is vital. If the world is going to be what is is. I would love to live in blissful distraction. I would love to live suspended in a nebulous cloud of play. Far from anxious paranoia and half–baked motives. This process of organizing sparked a memory. A thousand past lives ago, a female close to my age in my cohort addressed my lack of appreciation for pomp and circumstance. "Surprised to see you at this meeting. I didn't know you were still alive." I fired back my retort. I mixed one-part civility with two-parts quick-witted-snobbery. I was very impressed with myself. I had finally delivered a great comeback. It was served in the moment—not when I was trying to go to sleep later that night. I returned back to my kitchen. I now realize what I had missed. She was trying to flirt with me. I numbly watched my newly alienated coffee mug shatter at the end of its voyage to the kitchen floor. In my defense, I had no warning. What made me so unaware? She was trying to empathize. She was trying to tease me. She was trying to flirt with the person she thought I was. A rule breaker. A bad boy. Her timing was off. She caught me overly defensive. If people can't place you within their neat logical categories, you run the risk of being dismissed completely. Sometimes, by unknowingly dismissing yourself. I should have been her rule breaking bad boy. That is what I was supposed to be for her. I did not know. It wouldn't have worked out anyway.

I continued to organize. Scholarly works built up over the years. I re-imagined. Countless instances when my knee-jerk overcompensations made me completely unaware. I considered a few other instances. After a while, this process of self-analysis grew stale. I began reading into too much. Nothing warranted this level of analysis. This level of analysis that led to paranoia. This level of analysis that led to paralyzation. I must not have much going on in my life. This always happens. I was left with an inability to characterize myself. I wondered if I would get bored of me. It didn't matter. I was never going to live the way I wanted to. I was staring out the window. Again. I was never going to be in the place I wanted. With the people and things I wanted. Life is a period of perpetually coping with lost expectations before you don't exist for eternity. If I couldn't write out the life I wanted to love for myself, I could write it for another to read. I could paint it. I could film it. I could engineer it. I could build creatures to inhabit it. Etc. It would be my ideal life. Someone could have it. Even if it wasn't real for me. What would it look like?

I was at my lover who was not my lover's place. She was watching the news. The President who was not my President was finishing an announcement warning us about the war. Now he was addressing the sanctity of marriage. The importance of family values, religion, and mating for life with a member of the opposite sex. It was all horseshit to me. It was an agenda of pacification and profit margins. But for some reason my non-lover was not turning it off. "Aren't you going to change the channel?" She responded, "Actually, I think he has some good points. That's why I voted for him." I was paralyzed. The bait-and-switch. Or rather, the long hunt for the weakest/poorest sap on the planet, the slow weardown to near insanity, and the horrible surprise. I stammered, "You...you voted for him?" She calmly responded, "Oh, I didn't tell you? Yeah, I guess I changed my mind at the last second. My parents talked me into it. I guess I've changed my mind about a lot of things lately. I've been meaning to tell you." I looked toward the door. It was perfectly reasonable to leave. I wasn't the insane one. I was the sane one. I hadn't been brainwashed. She had. Who was this robot? Up until recently, she and I had shared similar views about this blathering idiot on the TV screen who would say anything to appease the lowest common denominator. "Oh." Was all I could muster. She responded, "Don't be too surprised. We all grow up sometime. It's just not practical to be overly idealistic." I tried staring into her eyes. I was attempting to glimpse any robot parts. She grew uncomfortable, "What? Don't look at me like that. So what, you're just going to be jobless and go unmarried the rest of your life? Don't you want a family?" There we go. Now we are getting to the point. This was about me dragging my feet to marry her. And probably about me being a loser. I wouldn't be as much of a loser if she wasn't attempting to drive me insane. But I didn't say anything. I still didn't want her to know I knew. I quickly deescalated the situation by pretending she had some good points. I was tired and hungry. And I wanted her to pay for dinner. In the end, I lost the logical thread to blame her. Don't we all leverage political stances for personal ends? To eventually achieve some greater purpose that most likely will get us laid? In her case—the objective was to be laid on a more permanent bases without having to share. I didn't agree with any of it. But at least I knew her motivation to support this idiot was paper thin. Or this was another part of her plan to drive me insane, as she would slowly convince me that she had held these political views all along.

At times it becomes necessary to think the opposite. When we are sane, we are functioning with 100% of our mental disorders. When we are mentally unstable it is because we are lacking one of the mental disorders that usually balances us out. The key is to figure out which mental disorder cancels out which mental disorder. Like a chemist making a stable compound.

All problems could be related. But one piece of the puzzle is missing. It defies a unifying theory. The equation remains (purposefully) unsolved.

Life itself is a moving target. Life is a living Being that does not want us to solve the problem. It does not want us to think of it as a problem. It does not want us to think there is a solution. This is why we can't know what happens when we die, why we never fully know ourselves, why we don't know if we are alone in the universe, why we can't solve world peace or hunger, etc. This could be for a very deep reason. Or because life is imperfect and it doesn't actually have a plan. It doesn't want us to know it doesn't have a plan and become more powerful than it. Like young parents trying to figure everything out for the first time. Or we don't have the answers because we purposefully hide them from ourselves. If we had the answers, we would cease to have purpose. We need problems to solve. We are a problem solving Being. We need wars to fight. We are a Being at war. Otherwise we aren't us. We are running from something. The fear of never being satisfied. The end of sanity for an individual. For a society. Or it is something else. Like robots or something.

I was watching the news. I came up with another word. Shissue: a shitty issue.

When I was younger. Days held a multitude of possibilities. I wanted to do everything. I remember waking up early to create newly designed paper airplanes. I checked out books from the library on salamanders. I was doing research. I had tasked myself with discovery. I was going to discover how to implant the glands that salamanders used to regenerate limbs into humans who had lost limbs. At first, my mother attempted to ration my tape supply for the planes I made. I could never understand this. The planes had to be made at any expense. Such a promising start. If it weren't for the life of pointless distractions that followed. I could have been a genius. No. I never stood a chance. Oh well.

"It's probably for the best." Everyone says. Their incessant refrain. One of the many ways to justify "fate." When we are left with no choice. A backwards way. A de-interaction with the universe. Perhaps the only way we interact. To envision life without the constant need to reassure one's place within it. What then? Perhaps the act of envisioning renders this impossible from the beginning.

To be outside oneself. The ability to become part of a different consciousness. To be fulfilled. Without anything for eternity. Without the ability to make sense. Without the ability to tell one's narrative. Without the ability to move. Without the ability to have one's Being reinforced. Without everything. Trapped within a coffin for eternity. To be comfortable with this situation. This is what occupied my thoughts in the past when my superiors lectured me for something that was beyond my control. We all knew it. They probably had nothing better to do. So I continued with my own thoughts. I have felt the anxiety of the eternal. It has an element of pure claustrophobic terror. Others must feel this as well. In their great works they attempt to guard us from it. Their efforts are noble. However, as seen in religion, people have taken the narrative literally. Narratives that were only meant to open up our consciousness. Instead of envisioning these narratives as the starting point, the readership built monuments. They lost the ability to escape at the appropriate moment. They lost the ability to accept the nothing of their existence. Monumental narratives do not allow us to practice dealing with the nothing of eternity. The great writers of the past thought our ability to interpret narratives would grow at the same rate as our ability to create systems of governance, develop technologies, sciences, etc. But something happened. We fixated on the wrong thing. We are not suited for eternity. We are not suited for right now. We are not suited for our past. We are lost in time. Time has lost us. We have lost ourselves.

The leading cause of death is being born.

Off the plane. Back visiting my parent's house. I found myself in newly hung pictures. "Everyone else looks complete." I remember thinking to myself. There is something missing about me. I couldn't completely person-ize the face I saw. I occupied a privileged position. I had an immediate knowledge. There was more to this person. More than this photo contained. I couldn't project onto the surface. Completely. I knew the incompleteness. We are that incompleteness. Most of the time. We are unwilling to see incompleteness in others. We only see our projection of them. When falling in love. We need to fully project onto the surface. We need to fully encapsulate them into a dream. I want to find another way to love. Sometimes people surprise us. We mis-predict the projection. It wanders outside our forward march. Sometimes we actually see them. Usually, we don't.

Our President who was not my President promised to be tougher on crime. He wanted to lock up more bad people. He wanted to keep them locked them up. Every day the police were growing more aggressive. I had no idea this was possible. They were already mistakenly killing innocent people every day. Or purposefully. I visited my home. It was changing. I met some old friends at a new bar. It was very nice to see them again. We had a couple drinks. We were too old to drink all night. I was waiting an obscene amount of time to close my tab. I asked if I could settle up. The bartender gave me attitude. Out of nowhere. The bouncer came over. He asked if I needed to leave. I told him I was trying to leave, but I needed to pay. He told me to calm down. I told him I was calm. He told me he didn't like my type. I didn't know what my type was. I told him I was trying to pay, so if he could leave me alone that would be great. He attempted to utilize his junior varsity wrestling moves. He attempted a full-nelson to take me outside. I easily slipped out of it. Because I could. He did not like this. He started to rush me. He was going to fight me now. Now every bouncer in the bar was going to fight me. Now the cops were going to fight me. However. To my credit, when the cops fought me, they put me in handcuffs. So I could only use my legs. Later, onlookers would tell me I did a pretty damn good job. Considering my odds. I was hit in the head early on. I suffered a concussion. I don't actually remember much of what happened. Just flashes. But it's a good thing the police showed up and took me to jail. Dangerous criminals like me can't be running around attempting to pay their bar tabs.

We are that Being that perpetually attempts to believe we are something other than an inevitable and temporary link in a long line of routine and necessary survival processes serving a greater purpose. This is the cause of much psychological confusion, pleasure, pain, etc. Narration is the way in which we attempt to disprove our ephemeral supporting role and generate reality. What else can we do? How much further can we go? If no further, can we unlearn it? We can backtrack. We can say we are one part of a larger process. However, we cannot unknow what we know. We know we are knowing (or at the very least trying to know) what we are telling ourselves that we know.

Sit quietly. Listen to what you are saying to yourself.

I was in a store later that week. For the past fifteen minutes I had been absent-mindedly smelling candles. Had anyone seen me do this? What kind of freak does this? I blushed. I looked around. Sheepishly. Nobody seemed to care. Nobody noticed. Nobody noticed anything. Only my major blunders. They always see those. I accredit this scent affinity to days of youth. Days spent accompanying my mother to various fabric stores, craft stores, gift stores, etc. My childhood. A stark romantic contradistinction. What has followed. Born to endless anxious night. The distinction stinks of romanticism. I'm now reminded. All my naïve attempts at being jaded. Proved to be all the more romantic. Merely in the opposite direction. When I was caught off guard. Some enchanting beauty. I forgot to be bitter. I'd melt. The sappiest idiot around. I really hate myself.

If I could re-create myself. I would build myself with some strange ephemeral fortitude. I would be a phoenix of a person. I would be eternally capable of imagining any fantastic reality. When I moved, the universe would move with me. My life would be a moonlit dance.

At the diner. I was reading an academic text on philosophy and society. I thought to myself. As the text helps provide more insight into my world, it simultaneously creates deeper divisions. Deeper divisions with the people in one's world. It provides more problems to have with the people in one's world. Is this a good thing? It is certainly prevalent. Does constructing and reconstructing the world and its problems help anyone?

Am I a horrible listener? When I am speaking, do others provide encouraging looks just to be polite? Are they actually telling me to shut up? How long does it take me, on average, to shut up about disappointing love affairs...five years, never? Maybe other people are the same? When my brother called a few minutes ago, I made a special effort to censor relationship monologues. I didn't complain about my dwindling career prospects. I didn't complain about my lack of success. I didn't complain about the high levels of stress, anxiety, depression, and paranoia compounded over the years. I imagine he was relieved. Nobody ever complained (to my face) about what must have been my incessant broken record babbling. My stupid anecdotes. Unknowingly repeated. Forcing embarrassment upon the listener for me. I have no other release valves. The pressure is too much. Oh well. To reward them, I promise myself. I will only open-up, if they do first. Even then, I will wait until they pry. Otherwise, I will only be a listener. This is my vow of silence. I will fail.

In High School I wrote a song for a girl. It was horrible. She loved it. Art is whatever gets you laid. She broke my heart.

A reoccurring thought plagued me. I couldn't shake it. The thought that I am already dead. The only thing keeping this afterlife from collapsing into a perpetual hellish reoccurring panic-attack-nightmare is my ability to conjure up and participate in the illusion of this pointless, meaningless, everyday life. This explained everything. Too clearly. This is why nothing ever improved. Why nothing ever changed. Except now I was terrified that I wouldn't be able to keep lying to myself. To keep the blinders of reality on by participating in so much busy-work, so much stupidity. I was terrified that I was no longer going to be able to save myself from the eternal hell of an ever-collapsing panic-attack where there is no forgetting, no safety, no relief, no illusion, no outside, etc. and so on forever.

You can survive anything.

Again, I thought. If only I could fill my mind with lofty thoughts. Thoughts that worked to change the world. Thoughts that focused on philosophical, mathematical, or scientific matters. I could actually get somewhere with my life. For the rest of the afternoon all I could think about was a girl. She snubbed me when I asked for her number at a bar last weekend. Next I made up a scenario where one of my superiors challenged me. They thought I had overlooked a crucial detail in a term paper I had written. I smartly fired back. Everyone was impressed. In real life, nobody is impressed. Ever. I would have never expected to be so grateful for pointless, repetitive, unhelpful, tiresome, inner-conversations. Lately my thoughts had become so existentially disturbing that I actually welcomed the return of these pointless conversations. They provided an obsessive anxiety, but at least there was that. At least I wasn't fading out into the nothingness completely.

I remember the past. Or I saw it in a movie. I was supposed to meet someone. They didn't show up. I was in an awkward part of town. It was an awkward time. I couldn't go back to work yet. I ate before I left. I went to a park. This was awkward. I sat their awkwardly. I watched the children. Awkwardly. People have children (consciously or otherwise) to half-relive those magical experiences of their youth. Their adult lives have lost all magic. To see, touch, and get lost in their own childhood. Again. I never want children of my own. I am unconvinced that bringing life into a world of death is not a mortal sin. But I know very little of death and even less of sin. I was thinking about this again before I decided to get stoned, later that night. I decided. I would only bring a child into the world (really a minor role on my behalf), if I had reached the conclusion that this world was a decent place and that life was worth living. With the war ragging everywhere, the police killing our own people, and decent people unable to make a living, there was little doubt that the world was currently not fit for children. I doubt I would ever reach the conclusion that life was worth living. I remember in a moment of drunken rage. Devastating embarrassment now. I told my father he had no idea what it was like to lead such a disappointing life. I told him I wished I had never been born. In that moment I meant it. In that moment I didn't mean it. But I also wished to have never existed. I thought the world and myself would have been better off had I never occurred. Especially after having said that. Since part of me didn't mean it. Part of me just wanted to make a point. Did it? I'm not sure anymore. Regardless. I have agreed with the sentiment since. Unfortunately. Almost immediately, I regretted those words to my father. No matter how true they were. The first part was a lie regardless. He did know regret. Who was I? Speaking for him? I was, and I am still, unimaginably sorry. The moment I uttered the phrase I realized it was the meanest thing I could have said to my father. If I were a super hero, my super power would be knowing the meanest thing I could say to another person. It's not a great super power. It does no good. Just harm. It was at that instant that I decided I would never become a father. At that instant, I was hit by the weight of bringing another life into existence. That weight would always be more than I could carry. If their life was going to be like mine. If I was merely bringing my own problems back into the world anew. Into a new lifeform. My question mark. Immovable. Whether life is a good in-and-of-itself. Whether or not a life lived is better than a life lived not at all.

A politician invoking the name of god is doing the work of the devil.

In the gap between sleeping and waking. I arrived at myself again. Myself as the person who perceives the world as consistent. Consistent with what? Consistent with the way it was before I went to sleep. How do I remember what that was like? I have no true trust. I can only feel the consistency of what usually occurs. Aside from this feeling and blurred memories, I have no reason. To think it could be otherwise. Something could tell me it is otherwise. So far, nothing has. Ever. Or maybe it has. Oh well. So it's merely me. Subjecting everything to the way I believe it should be. Until it isn't. And even then. Or is it another way entirely. Probably. It usually is. This isn't the way I originally thought this, or planned to write it out. What am I trying to ask? Did I wake up from the dream to come back to me? Or did I wake up from the dream in order to overpoweringly determine that the world is still as I have always thought it to be? Did I even wake up at all? Perhaps I died in my sleep? Perhaps I merely died in someone else's reality? In the life of a close friend, I no longer exist. How would I ever be able to figure that out? In the reality that I piece together every time I wake up (that I will into being), I'm alive. But in the reality that they will into being, I'm dead. I wonder what they wrote on my tombstone.

It was next Tuesday. Now a long time in the past. During a lecture I found myself drinking my coffee at the same pace as a colleague sitting across from me. Were we puppets tied to the same string? I found myself drinking my coffee at strategically irregular intervals. It did nothing to make me feel in control.

How will we react once we discover that life is one giant computer simulation or forgotten software program made by a higher-lifeform? What will we keep and what will we discard? About our lives? About our world? Will we all become computer programmers and attempt to hack the system in order to gain agency? Will we attempt a foolhardy search for life outside the computer system? Or are the current professions/daily tasks vital to "the program" in ways that we could never fully comprehend? For example, if someone were to leave a laundromat without their clothes, etc. What if the balance is disrupted? If the balance is disrupted, will our civilization and therefore all intelligent life get erased from just our planet or will the entire system shut down? Or will the system keep running and wait for intelligent life to reappear somewhere else in the universe? Of course, this assumes that the higher-lifeforms still manage the system. This assumes that the higher-lifeforms are still concerned with the system. How would our views on morality change? Would it turn into a free-for-all now that we've realized life is merely a game? However. Life always appeared to be game-like beforehand. Consider high school, etc. So why should anything change now that we are correct about the way life always already appeared to be? Would we realize this in time? Probably not. But we should realize that the meaning we project is merely the meaning we project. That ultimately (in the face of worse alternatives), we agree with the major rules and restrictions we placed on ourselves, which is why we placed them on ourselves in the first place (at least the useful ones). What will happen to god? The believers will keep on believing out of faith and habit as they always did. The believers who believed because it was fashionable and it aligned with their cultural surroundings will stop believing as their surroundings have changed. The non-believers will continue to not believe. Everyone who is born after this event won't consider these questions relevant. There is much they won't find relevant. Therefore, it's probably best they don't know. It's actually probably best that nobody knows any of this has taken place. It's not as if the physical laws of the game have changed. We are born. We die. If the physical laws change (the system/our biological code is hacked, etc.), this would of course bring on a whole new set of moral dilemmas. Again. It's probably best that we (the general public) are kept in the dark about the change in our world's physical laws as well. Unless we have a decent plan or understanding of what the next leap is going to look like. Top level government officials wouldn't even be let in on these secrets. The secrets would probably be kept by some secret society of highly intelligent and well-meaning garage scientists. This would probably be the best-case-scenario. Unfortunately, we all know it would be a multitrillion dollar corporation that would control this knowledge. Oh well.

You do something that you know is holding you back. Someone has pointed it out to you. You do it anyway. To spite them. Stop doing it. Today. Not for them. For you. Maybe you don't quit it forever. But see what happens. For now.

The dizzying late nights of laughter. Everyone is here. Everyone is celebrating nothing in particular. Consciousness ceases its tick-tock and transforms into woven impressions. Everyone forgets who they were trying to be and becomes who they are. I look around in romance.

In the past. In a certain time in my life. I was attempting to catch up to the week. All week. My life's re-occurring theme. Fighting on my heels. Lost in a flurry busy work. A flurry of inactivity. Nothing to show. No end-result. My existence was spent dealing in petty tasks. Anyone else could have dealt with these tasks. Possibly highly trained monkeys too. Maybe not so highly trained. Back at my pitiful apartment. I wasted this time haggling with my landlord. Medical bills. Insurance. Etc. While sleeping I kept waking up. I had been working for the higher-Beings again. All this work. Nothing gets accomplished. I work furiously. Only so I won't get screwed over as badly. Countless numbers of people and institutions. All taking my time, my money, and my headspace. I still get screwed over. At best I am able to momentarily imagine I'm not. Modern living does have some benefits. As we entwine ourselves with processes that bring nothing but trauma and anxiety, death becomes a much more pleasant experience. Instead of feeling sorry for those who have died, we will start saying, "Good for him, now he doesn't have to pay off his student loans." Instead of crying at funerals, people will clap and say, "Wish it was me!" If it's a suicide, they'll applaud the individual, "She did everything with such dedication!" and "I was always proud of how he followed through with every task he took on!" Death will become much more manageable as our society ventures further down this horribly visionless path it is hell-bent on taking. Everything has its benefits...that is one of the benefits of this model.

Looking into the past. Looking out to the stars. What are the odds that a past or a future exist for me out there? To escape into? To make decisions differently. Differently than I did in this time and place? This time around. What is big is small out there. Where everything collides. What will take me where I want to go?

I need to get out of my apartment. I heard myself say several years ago. I need to get of town. I was never programed for a sedentary lifestyle. One of the many reasons why my career path was a marriage of convenience. Since it was the end of the semester there wasn't an unbearable weight on my shoulders. Gnawing on me. Pushing me to frantically work on something. The ideal life. I was planning on living it one day. Some day. There would be constant adventure. But never the annoying inconveniences of adventure. For example, forgetting your toothbrush. I would edit out those parts. Even if I wrote them during a first draft. Like a film, I would just cut to the next scene when something annoying like that happened.

My lover who was not my lover agreed to watch her relative's dog. But we both knew what she had agreed to: I would watch her relative's dog. Although I previously determined I was completely unfit to be anyone's master, now I did not have a choice. It was the neediest dog in the world. It looked filthy. All the time. It needed human companionship at all times. I had to take it for walks constantly or it would claw away the door. It would climb into bed with us. It was the size of a small horse. It would lick itself all night long. I could not sleep. The loud dog slurps reverberated throughout the room. Every five minutes. This had to be a joke. My sleep had just started to recover. My lover who was not my lover must have sensed this. Therefore, the dog became a necessary step in her plan to slowly drive me insane. It was perfect. I couldn't report it to the police. Nobody would believe me. But it was just enough to disrupt everything once again. I was never going to be able to move forward in life. This must be true love.

One stupid struggle after another. There is no magic. Back to it. Could I recreate it? From scratch? These thoughts came in the ripples. A stone skipped in a brain left to spin. Announced from a gramophone. For all to hear but the sender. I was the sender. The sender who couldn't make sense of their own message. I thought of returning to Europe. Maybe for good. There was magic there. The cities were old. When I visited a lifetime of summers ago, I had no problem getting lost in streets where the buildings showed their age. I felt free. But no need to express it. To capture it. To shape it into space time. I dreaded the fact that I might be experiencing it artificially. But I chalked this up to my typical paranoia. I forced it away. I did not let it cheapen my experience. I was at peace with this artifice. Also, I think being drunk helped put a fade on the paranoia and over-analysis. I was left in a beautiful impressionistic European dreamscape. The alcohol also explains how I got so lost.

There is no center.

Later that night I thought about a night many nights ago. I was on a date with a girl I had been seeing—unfortunately not all of her. I looked down. We were holding hands. I looked up. We were walking along the downtown waterfront. Bridges cast shadows on the black water aflame with the lights of the city. It felt like we were in a perfume advertisement. It was perfect. Too perfect. She was beautiful. This is what lovers do. It was too much what lovers did. I was trapped in a perfume Ad for all of eternity with a beautiful girl. I was too distracted by the perfection. I felt claustrophobic. Trapped in that perfect moment. Forever. Eternity. The name of the perfume: "Eternity...stay in the moment forever." The night ended. She was too busy to see me again. Because of work. So I never saw her again. Until a few years later. I saw her at a mall. In a city. We were both passing through. She was married to a nerdy looking man who was far less attractive than she was. He was very socially awkward. Maybe true love really does exist. Maybe true love is blind. Maybe true love extends beyond mere physical attraction. They didn't even attempt to fake it. They couldn't stand each other. Never mind. I tried to pretend I was interested. I doubt I was convincing. I doubt she cared. She was overly friendly. She kept saying we (she included my imaginary spouse who didn't exist) should all try and get together sometime to "reconnect." She said this would be "fun" for everyone. Her persistent invitations made the situation more awkward. She was very persistent. We exchanged information once again. I gave her a fake number. I wonder when they'll start making a perfume named Divorce. What would that smell like? Cash and liquor.

Frustration. When I fail to adequately describe my projects. This compared to the satisfaction in creating them. Others cannot see. They cannot see until the finished product is complete. Only then (and in the right mood) do they have a chance at the "Aha! Moment." When the original purpose is revealed. Is this how god or consciousness or inspiration or the higher-power feels? They are not very good at explaining themselves, daily life, pain, injustices, the justification for success, the catastrophe, the unconscious. However, there are times when the picture becomes complete. All is revealed at once. Not logically. Not singularly. Not morally. In its vision. As it is. Is it necessary for everything to be concealed in order for it to be unconcealed? Or is this an oversight on their part?

We are impressed by all the wrong things.

I was looking out a window. Again. Or was I waiting in line? I forget. But I remember thinking the following. Looking through the eyes of others to see one's self. Not a flattering task. It does not provide instant happiness. The happiness of an unquestioning singularly blissful self. It does allow the individual to do things they wouldn't be able to do otherwise. Maybe one can find solace in that? It does cause uncertainty. Perhaps this is not necessarily a bad thing. Maybe it is? Maybe blind certainty and trusting one's self is all there is. Whether the individual is wrong matters very little. Nobody is actually right or wrong in the end? All that matters is one's enthusiasm. All that matters is that they put all of themselves into their task. This is the only measure we are judged by. What to do? Let's rewind. Let's say the self-reflexive path is the one we have taken. Being uncertain of oneself is a good thing. While this does not lead to dumb blissfulness, the individual merely needs to learn how to derive a new kind of pleasure. A pleasure that is very different from the supposed pleasure that others may or may not derive from remaining unaware. Remaining unaware might be great in a vacuum. Remaining unaware might not be great in a world of actions, reactions, actors, and factors who are more than willing to take advantage of this unawareness. The individual takes on a burdening stress when they take on the viewpoints of others. More so when they have to see themselves through this view point. More so if they aren't merely playing a passing devils advocate: merely defeating the one-dimensional others swimming about in their heads. It is heavy. What is it all worth? This is the wrong question. How does it get put to use? Also the wrong question. The individual needs to make oneself available. This might be the key. Or another dead-end. Oh well.

I was looking out the window. A short fat robin hopped around the grass. He was squawking at the other robins. The other robins ignored him. He reminded me of our high school football coach. He thrived on small town fame. He wanted to be the big fish in the small pond. He demanded 100% enthusiasm for the cause. For his way of doing things. If you didn't believe he was god, you didn't have to say anything. He could smell it. His player could murder someone, and he would forgive them and start them the next game, so long as they apologized and genuinely believed in his system. But if he smelled a whiff of dissension, disbelief, or if he simply looked into the eyes of an adolescent, and he saw the faintest glimmer of conscious critical thought, he would bench you the rest of the season. No matter how good you were. No matter how much it hurt the rest of the team. No matter how many games we lost. Never mind, the short fat robin that was squawking angrily at anything that moved in the front yard was much more noble and far more successful than our high school football coach.

All the creative types. All the big imaginations. In the past their focus was on incredible technological solutions. They built the pyramids. They created new forms of government. They radically changed music, medicine, painting, architecture, science, etc. They created fire and civilizations. They are now working for advertising firms making car and cellphone commercials. Imagine if a space alien came down to earth. Before they do anything else, the space alien enters a store selling televisions. They witness a cellphone commercial. The aliens exclaim: "What glorious news! These Earth people must be so excited! This 'remarkable technological accomplishment' this, one of 'humankind's crowning achievements,' this 'the next big thing,' is said to 'change everyone's life forever'!" The space alien would ask the person next to them, "How might I acquire such a cherished object?" The person would respond, "Oh I already have one. It's kinda of shitty."

People are more calculative than you think. People are less calculative than you think. No matter what you think, you will be wrong. We project so much drama onto others and their situations. We are completely wrong. We are exactly right. We have no way to tell. Even if we are right, and we confront the person about the issue, they will lie to us. They don't want to give us the satisfaction of being right. Or if it's too personal, they will give us a false answer. If we are wrong, they won't want us to feel bad for being an idiot. Or if they care too much about us, they would rather we weren't embarrassed than the story be told correctly. Or if they want to sleep with us, they will tell us we are right. But really we are wrong. And these are the results we build our world out of. Oh well.

We are all terrified of how terrifyingly boring life can be. We don't fear death. We fear being bored to death.

I was pointlessly vacuuming my perpetually dingy apartment. It was just going to get dirty again. I thought about an incident with my little brother. He was goofing around. He was brandishing a toilet plunger as a sword. The plunger swung around touching everything. Being the germaphobe I was, I angrily told him, "That's been in the toilet! What are you doing?!" The joyous look immediately faded from his face. He was trying to be funny for his older brother. He was embarrassed. Maybe he hadn't realized the actual use of the plunger. Maybe he assumed the adults thoroughly cleaned it between uses. I immediately felt like the worst person in the world. If I could have one wish it would be that this experience did not have any detrimental effects on the person he would become.

Far stranger and inadmissible than theft, murder, rape, or suicide. I quit everything. I lived in isolation for two years. Nobody understood why I did this. It went against everything. I told everyone my plan. They recommend various institutions. For help. I refused. They threatened to involve the law. They threatened to call the police. They would put me on a missing person's list. They did this out of love. I knew this. I can't say it was the best time of my life. Parts of it were no fun at all. My company was my solitude. Interactions with the passing stranger were brief and uneventful. The only years of my life lived in the moment. Aware of the present. This is actually very difficult to do. It made me uneasy. Especially at the beginning. I thought the most important thoughts of my life. I never wrote them down. My disconnection revealed the pointless connectivity spreading us thin. Monumental distraction. We generate most of our unhappiness by constantly failing to catch up with ourselves. The kinetic energy of expectations. The sheer magnitude of the spider web we have woven ourselves into. Too many potential arguments to take up. During this time, I did not get worked up about things I usually get worked up about. I was easier. I had no timelines. If I were in the real world, I would have cared very little if the car in front of me took extra time to get moving. I got a very basic job that paid very little money. I didn't buy much and lived very inexpensively. I was very bored most of the time. I understand why we need distractions. It doesn't sit well with me. There is no way to live that is better than any other way to live. It's all the same. In the end, there is no point in taking a break if you can never leave for good. Only the dead know if you can leave for good.

My only power: my ability to refuse to take the world seriously. To do the very thing everyone believes I would never do. Give up all power. No matter how little. Give up the belief there is such a thing as power. This undermines everything.

The other night I had a vivid dream. There was nobody I could turn to. I alone was left to piece everything together. I started making giant billboards. I wrote questions on banners and attached them to planes. I included contact information. I received very few responses. The few responses I did receive were from: an author writing a book on a similar topic, a professional athlete, an elderly couple who were professors, an actress, and a rich entrepreneur/inventor. The author said he didn't know what else to do about these questions. He only wrote his stories in the hopes that others would contact him. His motive: prove there is intelligent life in our society. He planned on building a team of individuals to help him figure out this mess of a reality. So far, he only received fan mail and paychecks (he didn't mind either). The professional athlete started to realize reality was not as it seemed to be. Every game appeared to be fixed. Regardless of what he did. The college professors tried publishing papers about similar situations. They tried teaching courses on both the theoretical aspects and scientific aspects. They soon found themselves banned from every journal and every university for being too radical. The actress tried to express her views publicly. Everyone either assumed she was high or she felt entitled to behave irresponsibly. Her promising career tanked. The rich entrepreneur was wealthy and disconnected from the world before he stared having these realizations. Initially, he didn't feel the need to do anything about them. Eventually we all met. The messages I sent out had been the catalyst. At a certain point in our adventures, I realized the high probability that all of us were simply insane. It was impossible to rule out. Each of us had reached this conclusion on our own. Eventually we decided against telling anyone outside the group about "the way things really were" because nobody would believe us. Also, as of yet, we didn't have a way out of it. We didn't have a better dream. It wouldn't do any good to wake everyone up from the current nightmare. We also realized we might be a cult. But we all agreed we would never join a cult. We all lived in the rich entrepreneur's mansion during this time. It was a paradise. It comprised the latest technological advances with fantastic natural wonders. I couldn't tell if the flamingos were robots. During our time together we all agreed on a few ground rules. We thought the higher-powers, or machines, or gods (or whoever was running this thing) had the infinite wisdom to create a multiverse but was not stupid enough (as we are) to come up with reasons for why this vast simulated game was supposed to be played in the first place. So they rely on us to come up with these reasons. This superior force has put us in a state wherein we are perpetually unable to fully understand how, when, where, and why the game is being played. Yet, they are hoping they will be able to lead us into creating good enough reasons for why everything should exist the way it does. They want to be able to figure it all out a fraction of a second before we do. But we never can. Or, in other words, everything we have come up with has been shit. Therefore, the game goes on. Our stupidity is saving us. Or it is preventing us from becoming one with our higher-power. We could never figure that part out. Oh well. On several occasions we attempted to contact this higher-lifeform. We wanted to work with them, not against them. With everyone's talents and the entrepreneur's unlimited resources, we almost succeeded. We thought we received messages back via a complex pattern of hyper-laser Morse code that was transmitted through a satellite we launched. After several formal greetings and a little back-and-forth, we deduced that there was a high probability we were communicating with the alien equivalency of a prank phone call. The transmission cut out right after they sent us what we translated to be a very dirty joke. After a while things starter to fall apart. Nothing seemed to work. We weren't getting anywhere. The government started to put us on various watch lists. We could hardly leave the mansion without being harassed. The mansion started to get vandalized. Bad publicity was being widely circulated about us. I started to fall in love with the actress. Of course she fell in love with the jock. The elderly professor couple fell in love with me. And so, of course, I left. We all parted on semi-good terms (all things considered). We knew the project had a ticking clock. I think each of us kept working on the problem individually. Probably for the rest of our lives. I lived out the rest of my life. It was all right. Nothing got too great. Nothing got too bad. But on my death bed I finally had the answer. I finally had my great big idea. My big contribution. I finally realized what everything had been building towards...and then I woke up. I was incredibly disappointed. Oh well.

Always look for what you're not looking for.

To face my mortality. I had to become myself. Imperfect and incomplete. Not ideal. Not what I had in mind. What happened to be there. At the time. That's what I was going to be. That's what I am. I got a tattoo. Marking my impermanence. Accepting my possible mistake. Taking a step toward identification. Having style. A step away from the perfection of non-identity. From nothing ness. From a perspective able to take in everything at once. Not judge. Not decide. Not be a self. No personality, religion, science, laws, art, culture, or language. To be outside of space and time. But this is a luxury I was not afforded. I stumble forward. I live my decisions with regret. With my style I will eventually hate. With modernity. Years passed. Minutes passed. I hate them. My decisions. I was their prisoner. I better start owning them. I should start to wear them. They will be my style. I have been avoiding them. I have been avoiding decisions. I have been avoiding becoming me. I still wanted to be the pure vision. It will never happen. So I must be me now.

I was tricked into another family gathering. I waited in line for food. Out of my element. Away from my compatriots. Luckily my thoughts were still able to wander. We need to put corporations in charge of educating our children. The only way to motivate people is to pay them money. We need to provide cash incentives for these children to learn. The better they do in class the more money they will receive. But what are these corporations going to get in return for paying our children to work harder in school? The kids could make stuff when they study. But because they aren't very smart yet, they can just make simple things like clothes and shoes. And the kids wouldn't be smart enough to unionize, so we don't have to pay them very much money. Some parents are probably going to get jealous that their kids aren't making as much money as other kids. But you know what? Their kid is just going to have to try harder. It's all about incentives. Maybe someday, they too can put a bumper sticker on their car that states "My Kid Made 5 Million Units and Earned $10 in the Sweat Shop this Year." I mean, "at School this Year."

Nobody thinks of me as a perfectionist. I don't either. Anymore. I never wanted to be a perfectionist. I merely wanted to do a decent job. I can't even do that. My endeavors turn against me. Especially if others are involved. The outcome turns haphazard. This acts as no relief to the dictator styled order I attempt to impose on the universe. Only to see it fail every time. Nobody thinks of me as an organized individual. The world perpetually turns to chaos around me. This acts as no relief to the saintly styled order I attempt to impose on the universe. Only to see it fail every time. Oh well.

We couldn't stop killing each other on a regular basis. One of the most popular ways we accomplished this is with our vehicles. Our President told us that he was putting more police on the streets to issue traffic tickets. This did nothing to prevent us from killing each other with our cars. Our intelligence was limited. The cars were fast. Physics was simply not on our side. Surely nothing bad was going to happen to us in a car. Statistics were not on our side. My lover who was not my lover and I went for a road trip in her car. I was driving. She had too many tickets on her record. In this particularly ultra conservative area the billboards advertised three things: 1. Fireworks, 2. Peaches, 3. Adult Superstores. What makes the store super? Probably their selection and the amount of products they sell. What makes the store adult? Sex products. I'm not sure why they didn't think to combine all three into one mega ultra super store. Maybe it's best to keep fireworks separate from the other similarly shaped objects. The peaches would have been a good fit. I'm sure space aliens would be somewhat confused: they would arrive at the Adult Superstore looking to purchase fully grown humans. The aliens would also experience a great deal of confusion when they discovered that the distinction "Adult" does not always translate to "sexual." For example, they would show up to the local Adult Education Center expecting a raunchy "how-to" sexual-workshop. Instead, they would have disappointingly signed up for educational classes. During the road trip, unconcerned and undereducated drivers whizzed past me reaching speeds well over the speed limit. They changed lanes with reckless abandon. They rode each others bumpers and almost got into several wrecks. A car shot past me. "That guy is going to get pulled over." I saw flashing lights in my rearview mirror. "See." I was pulling over to let the cop get by me. But it turns out he was pulling me over. He gave me a ticket for going five miles over the speed limit. I asked him, "Did you see the car pass me travelling way over the speed limit? Why didn't you pull him over? Why did you pull me over?" He replied, "I don't like your type. Now if your going to get mouthy, I'll drag you out of your car, beat you, and if your still alive, I'll take you to jail. How'd you like that?" I still don't know what my type is. Why do these people hate it so much?

Different path trajectories stretch across the parallel universe. I am furthest from the one I was supposed to take. The other trajectories use my trajectory in dreams to help them. But my own trajectory is the wrong one. Every decision I have made has been the wrong one. It had to be. It brought context to the other trajectories. It allowed them to learn the lesson without having it effect their trajectory. They live vicariously through my trajectory. Some people never appear to make mistakes. They are living their right trajectory.

I've never been married. But more impressively, I've never been divorced. It's not marriage I'm afraid of. It's the divorce I don't have time for. I don't have to be married to know what a horrible idea it is. I already know it's a horrible idea because of the con married people attempt to run on non-married people. They've built a society attempting to punish those who live free and single. They hate to see other people happy.

So they construct holidays to celebrate couples. These holidays make single people feel lonely. They don't actually make couples feel any better about their relationship. Typically, they are a point of high stress and anxiety for couples. There are major monetary benefits for being married. Single individuals are monetarily penalized and it isn't socially acceptable to be single. Especially long into one's life. If an individual is single for long there must be something wrong with them. When it comes to the wedding ceremony, married couples approach the bride-and-groom-to-be and tell them, "You should have a party to celebrate your wedding." The future married couple asks, "Okay should we have a few friends over at our place?" The married people respond, "No, no. You should invite everyone you know: friends, family, everyone. You should spend a lot of money, rent an expensive venue, cater great food and alcohol, hire live-music, purchase expensive rings for each other, and ask a priest to be there when you exchange said rings. But most importantly make sure that the government validates the marriage as a legally binding contract, otherwise, one of you might think about getting out of it too easily." The couple-to-be asks, "Wait why would we ever do that?" The response: "Because you're never going to be happy ever again. The only pleasure we get is seeing you idiots make the same stupid mistake we did." The happy couple confusedly replies, "Wait, we thought getting married and having kids was the best experience one could have." The others respond, "No, doing psychedelic drugs is the best experience you can have. We tell you that getting married and having kids is the best experience you can have because if we didn't, nobody in their goddamn right minds would ever get married and have kids...and the human race would die out. Look at how heavily we have to pressure others into this nightmare. Look around you at all the propaganda we have to constantly put out in order to brainwash people into believing that procreation is a good idea. Trust us, it's not. It's the fucking worst."

Nothing became of me. It wasn't for lack of trying. I left nothing in the tank. Nothing for the journey back. And I failed. Or was I saving it all for one final push? I feel the window turning into a wall. And so I did nothing. I wasted my years. According to some, I was talented. Or they were lying to me. If they were telling the truth, the talent I had, it had nowhere to go. I had no mentor to develop it. No career came along to compliment it. No peer group to support it. I am sure there were many others like me. Our time would never come. For no reason at all. Simply because we chose to live in a world that favored a system of nepotism with a hint of arbitrary random chance that we pretended did not exist but which we purposefully self-imposed and then pretended that we were all-purposeful and all-knowing. The world got what it deserved. It got war. Its stock markets crashed. They put the wrong people in charge. I am sure, in time, humanity was able to at least solve this problem, or at least get rid of careers altogether and establish humanity's talents around another center of purpose. Something outside the artificial time restraints and narrative expectations we perpetually self-imposed on ourselves and others.

Christmas at my Grandparent's. Old-growth forests. Tchaikovsky and rain. The smell of cigar smoke. A brick fireplace. Dark leather armchairs. Mass. Beautiful and Catholic. Dark wooden pews. White marble floors. Lofty church arches. Stained glass. A beautiful blonde girl with a ponytail. Summers. Freshly cut grass. I'm trying desperately to re-create a dream. This dream will save me from myself. This dream will save me from the darkness on both sides. What happens when we grow old? What can make us feel again?

We keep living the same life. When we die we are reborn. We forget what happened during the last life. This explains why our intuitions can be correct. Or at least, why we feel as if our intuitions can be correct. But we forget the outcome of the previous life. So we are just as likely to guess wrong. Unless we have lived through the cycle several times before. This explains déjà vu's. When we die, we can't remember doing it previously. Some people are more practiced and more aware that they've done it before. This helps them in their decisions the next time around. It can also hurt them. They may lack enthusiasm and feel like the game is rigged. Have I said all this before? Oh well.

Our fearless leader, our President who was not my President has reset our priorities. Comparatively, our children are being out preformed in school. Therefore, the only logical solution is that we need to spend more on our military. Because once everyone else becomes better than us at everything, we still need to be able to bomb the fuck out of them. For, if

I was our President, I would famously state, "The only thing we have to fear is...ourselves."

Even though we are merely operating within a game that is rigged by higher-Beings, it wouldn't hurt to create new value systems. We have yet to establish value systems that don't work through exclusion: moving everything into overly neat dichotomies and hierarchies at the expense of others. Certain works of art allow us to consider creating new value systems. Value systems that defy value and systems. Here we would not fixate on specific highly formulaic moments but expand our consciousness into other realms.

When we realize our reactions to a situation were due to false information. When we realize our opinions were supported by an untrustworthy individual. When we realize our actions were determined by an undiagnosed mental disorder. When we wake up from a night of mayhem and reflect on what drugs, alcohol, or our own unbridled passions brought out of us. All these instances combined could not brace us for the jolt we would feel if we were to collide with a previously undetectable force. A force that reveals its control of the predetermined pathways we wander.

I forgot to get milk at the store. I went back to the store. The expiration date on the milk made me realize the end of the month. Where did time go? My expiration date. All the years I would never see. What a funny way to measure time. The way a week looks as you visualize it. A geometric shape. Does the concept of a week have a smell too? A sound? Somehow I knew how it felt to die. Or maybe I had no idea. I wonder if I had done it before. It feels like I have. Stabbed. In a very vivid dream I was executed. On my knees. Hands tied behind my back. Gun to my head. Bang. I died for something. When I was asleep with a high fever, I felt myself being lifted up and away from my body. I was turning into a tree that was soon going to become the sky. Starting from the base of the tree escaping through to its outermost branches. But I told the force taking me away, "Not yet. Not Yet." And I sank back down. Becoming myself again. Waking up, I realized my fever had spiked to a dangerous level. During a very intense and disturbing panic attack, suicide was quickly becoming the only way out. The un-spoken voices where saying something to the effect, "It's time for you to see everything. It's time for you to join us." I told them "Not yet. Not yet." And the intensity stopped. During the onset of what probably would have been a full seizure, I felt an invisible hand forcefully pushing my head. I started to fall out of my chair and was slowly moving closer and closer to the floor. Resist the hand. I thought to myself. Push back. And I avoided being dissolved into the floor. In all these instances the force was not passive. It was not neutral. It was the same force but also different. I was fighting. Negotiating. Bargaining. But I don't know for what. I live in fear of the time when there will be no bargaining. Had I spoken to death or was it merely reminding me what it could do to me?

I found myself a prisoner. Once again. Cornered at a family event. Someone was graduating. Someone was about to have life's bandages ripped off. Wounds would be exposed. Old and new. "Best of luck," I said. I meant it. Then cornered. By a non-exile. Someone other than a very old or very young person. They wanted to talk to me about sports. I wanted to talk about how to rig a game. I was planning on talking about it with myself. They were interrupting. This was not what they wanted to talk about. I had enough drinks in me not to care. I plowed through my one-sided conversation. It wasn't so much about how sports were rigged (this should already be assumed), but how you could rig any game in general. But for their sake, I tried to stick with the sports metaphor. I believe it went as follows. First of all, everything depends on how deeply you have infiltrated the game beforehand. If you have players who will do things for you, then you have fewer variables to manage. If you have coaches who will do things for you, then you have more variables to manage, but not as many as if you only have referees who will do things for you, etc. If you are only at the level of referees, then here are some guidelines. In order to rig a game, the game has to be close enough to be rigged. One team can't be completely dominating the other team. Also, the team you are trying to rig for has to break through and win the game. Nothing looks worse than attempting to rig a game and having the team you are rigging for lose. That's when it becomes obvious. The rigging should never happen at the last second. That is the work of an amateur. That will also make it overly obvious. Sometimes these things can't be avoided. Remember that you are working against the undeniable will and spirit of one team or individual. Their passion to win often works against unimaginable odds. They will do remarkable, mind blowing things to win. You need to prevent this. Sometimes you can't, so you will have to make mistakes, and make obviously bad calls at the end of games, etc. In short, your job is to make small calls throughout the game, but even more so, your job is to NOT make calls. It's not about the calls you make, it's about the calls YOU DON'T make that matter. These will draw far less attention to yourself. You can always say that you didn't see something happen. You can always turn a blind eye. You can always blame it on human error to NOT see something happen. You can always say that you were just "letting them play." Especially at the end of the game. Ranking systems are your best friend. They help make up for your mistakes. The more convoluted the ranking system the easier it is to help cover up the rigging of games. The best ranking system is the ranking system whose logic is circular. This allows you to justify biasing the ranking system towards the result you desire. Take, for example, this argument to prove that a conference is good and therefore justify ranking the teams in that conference higher than the teams of another conference: "This team is good. Why is this team good? Because they play in this conference. Why is this conference good? Because this team plays in it." This can be developed further during the season to show why one conference is strong and why another conference is weak: "Why is this conference strong? Because the competition is fierce. Top teams often get dethroned by bottom teams. Why is this conference weak? Because the conference is unstable. Top teams often get dethroned by bottom teams." When the rankings come out, the analysts don't even need to be in on the rigging. They will create the narratives you want them to create. The analysts are looking to justify the rankings because they want to appear as if they understand what is going on. They do not want to look like idiots. They want to prove to the world that they understand the logic of the rankings. But it's not a perfect system. Teams that you don't want to make it through will still make it through. This is why, at the administrative level, you need everyone to be in your pocket at all times. You need the ability to do random drug testing. The drugs need to be legal-ish in some instances and not in others. You need the ability to call into question bad recruiting practices that everyone does. You need the ability to call into question bad fundraising practices that everyone does. You allow all of them to violate all the rules. You expect them to violate the rules. You encourage them to violate the rules. The game requires them to violate the rules. You need to have every individual or every team violating the rules. At anytime you need to be able to call in favors if need be, silence anyone if need be, threaten to call people out if need be, cut funding if need be, impose sanctions if need be. Everyone is cheating. Everyone knows this. In order to rig the game well, you should take care of as much business off the field as possible. On the field, the game needs to look as natural as possible. On the field, you should manage as little as possible. The winners need to have the biggest fan base. These fans need to buy the most apparel. The most tickets. They need to be the least analytical and most willing to accept that their team won due to their natural abilities. They usually come from the most boring places. They usually have nothing else that is very meaningful in their lives. But not always. But usually. And many years you simply need to mix it up so that the fans (who take these things way too seriously and follow these things way too closely) don't figure it out. When you start to see the eyes of the larger population glaze over in boredom, you have to stop playing the hits. They are starting to figure it out. But don't be too worried. At the end of the day. They are always powerless. The most important thing are the larger economic gains. This is always a matter of economy. This is a matter of national security. Global investors have stock in this. This is not merely television contracts and shoe contracts. Although, of course, it is those things as well. We are talking about being able to calculate the economic sweet-spot, align it with the best narrative and the most active fan-base, and choose the winner accordingly. At that point, I believe my listener zoned out completely. I was confused. I thought I was just now talking about sports again. Something they were interested in. Oh well.

So assured. In hindsight. Given the chance to do it all over again, I imagine I'd do the exact same thing 99.9% of the time. For worse or for worse. If you were granted the ability to relive part of your life, there are some things you'd want to change. At the same time, there is much you have achieved. You'd want to accomplish it once again. So you'd try to make yourself as aware as possible of the steps you took to get where you got. It would drive you insane. So do you make the same general decisions, or do you make different ones? How do you know if what you did was luck or skill? Perhaps the second time around things end up far worse? You misunderstand what led you to be successful the first time around. Your alleged meager level of success was actually obtained by battling outstanding odds. You did not appreciate this. The second time around you fail to accomplish what you assumed were meager goals. Or the second time around life is a million times better and everything is much easier. I guess you won't know. Oh well.

You know someone who is suffering. Don't try to know why they are suffering. Don't try to know their suffering. Just know they are suffering. That is all you need to know. Now you know what to do.

During a job interview my mind wandered. I imagined this scenario: god calls its publicist into its office. God says, "Listen, I'm grateful about this bible and everything, but couldn't we have gotten someone else to write it? I'm looking into the future and I see all these great writers who haven't even emerged yet. Can't we just wait for one of them? I mean these guys right now are fine, but they're a bunch of hacks compared to what will come later. I feel like the book simply won't age well. Once individuals who abuse my teachings for political-ends are called out, people will start to realize these stories are incredibly dated and have no bearing on any advanced morality. The people will realize they've been projecting too much onto old texts that are poorly constructed, selected, translated, and simply not universal." God's publicist responds, "People will read anything. Don't give them too much credit."

The problem remains. I'm basing everything off of my ability to make sense of the world. If that ability is faulty. If that ability is marginally miscalibrated. Everything is a catastrophic miscalculation. The reason I do not get any of the jobs I apply for: I'm simply not good enough. I never arrive at this conclusion. I make up other reasons. The misconceptions I have about my talents. Illusions of the highest degree. They are all misinterpretations of feedback from others. I only listen to those who I already agree with. I dismiss those who I already disagree with. There is no way for me to make any sound judgments about anything because I am no longer capable of making sound judgments about everything. There is no longer any way for me to tell that there is no longer any way for me to tell. I've successfully removed all indicators that I am on the wrong path. Even as

I type this, it doesn't seem like a big deal. What else is there to do? Either way, I have no other options. Oh well. Whether I do something or don't do something, the outcome is always the same. Whether I think one way or don't think one way, the outcome is the same. I have no ability to judge if an outcome is good or bad. I have no ability to differentiate an outcome from the process leading up to it. Being a ghost isn't so bad. You can yell as loud as you want. Nobody cares.

A long time ago, I caught one of my girlfriends looking at pictures of her and her ex-boyfriend. They were on a tropical vacation together. We were stuck in her apartment. In the dead of winter. During finals week. A short time passed. She got mad at me for spending too much time in her apartment. Her place was closer to the university. This is why we spent more time at her place. Now she was kicking me out. I was going back to my place for the night. She told me not to go. A short time passed. After the school year, she decided she was going to move back in with her parents. Back to her hometown. I still didn't know what I was going to do. A short time passed. We went out to dinner. I came back from the restroom. She had been texting. She quickly put her phone underneath the table. I pretended not to notice. I ended up breaking up with her. I had to survive finals week. I had to be a human again. She got married soon after. To someone else. Some people are lucky I guess. The funny thing is, we were passionately in love.

Can a distinction be made between those who know this life is a simulation created by a higher-power, and those who don't know? I was back at the pet store. The relatives of my lover who was not my lover recently picked up their terrible dog. I was not on the market to purchase a pet. I was simply at the pet store. Watching the fish in the tank. I was trying to determine if any of them understood their plight. None of them held my gaze. Was this their ignorance or mine? These fish. These humans. Unware, the distinction cannot be made. Instead, the overly paranoid among us provide a better dividing line. Not just humans. But dogs. The one I had been watching for my non-lover. The dog would bark at the wind. Incessantly. These paranoid creatures made a pact with the higher-power. We chose to live our life-cycles forever instead of dying off like the others after their first life-cycle (the normals). The normals become simulations after their first life-cycle. The trade-off is that they are played by the higher-power for entertainment purposes. As in our world of entertainment, we put on a pair of virtual reality glasses, they inhabit the bodies of the normals and play them as a game. Meanwhile the normals go on living uninterrupted while several of the higher-powers could be playing them at once. This would explain why some of us feel so out of touch with ourselves. This would explain why some of us turn to writing far-fetched theories about reality. But our wild speculations only further distract us from what is going on. The only opportunity to maintain some control is when we paradoxically have our guard down. When we are drunk, high, etc. We effectively shut down the overly logical game playing paths we force ourselves to adhere to out of our fear of the unknown. This fear keeps us in check. Currently we are on about the millionth life-cycle simulation and very rarely do the normals become vaguely aware that things aren't working out the way their original self would want them to work. And currently we are on about the millionth life-cycle simulation and very rarely do the normals become vaguely aware that something is not right. This is why they make decisions they typically would not make. The Beings inside them want to make other decisions while playing the game. The simulation overrides their ability to fully understand that they do not want to make this decision. They make up reasons after the fact as to why they made the decision they made. There is a buffer. The buffer works like the lag on a live television feed to prevent cursing from reaching the sensitive puritanical ears of the docile American family. The lag is the false belief in cause and effect. It works in tandem with the normals habitual and perpetual reinforcement of traditions. They have no knowledge of the origins of these traditions. All of this prevents them from understanding their lack of agency in the decisions they think they make. However, a mischievous higher-Being got bored and started to play the game of "me." They thought it would be funny to have me write all this down. I already had a considerable amount typed out from when I was drunk, stoned, and otherwise out of my mind. They decided to let me go for it when I was sober as well. No one will read it though. Oh well.

What was I doing wrong? Love is a game everyone is good at playing but me. Until I talk to other people. Now I remember. They are bad at it too. Okay, never mind. Everyone is bad at it.

Several hundred years ago, I entered the office of the acting Head of the Department. Emphasis on acting. He fit right in. I asked if they offered a particular set of courses to students over the summer semester. I hadn't been able to teach these courses in my first years of graduate school. They were my specialty. Teaching these courses would look good when I applied for jobs. I never found out the answer to my question. Instead he managed to devolve the conversation into a strange personal competition between he and I. He challenging me to explain why, when I went on the job market, I would be hired to teach these courses over someone else from a specific ivy league school (that he happened to attend). At first I thought he was joking. It would have been a really good joke. He was not joking. I told him exactly why I would be hired over those individuals. He was not expecting me to have reasons. He was not expecting me to have good reasons. He suggested I assemble the other graduate students in our program, ask a professor, and organize a graduate course for us to take on the subject. I told him I was done with my course work. We sat in awkward silence. I offered him no way out of this silence. He thought the silence would make me nervous. He was wrong. I loved it. He recommended I stop by the office of his secretary next door to see if there were any more entry-level courses available to teach over the summer. I had already taught these courses. I did not need to teach them again. I said I would. On my way out, I made sure he noticed me walking past his secretary's office. Luckily, everybody lost that day. Especially the students. Oh well.

Far worse than attending your own family function: attending someone else's family function. My lover who was not my lover somehow tricked me into a weekend trip to visit her family. I still don't understand how she accomplished this feat. I believe I was drugged. Or I simply misheard her and thought we were going to lunch. They were not outright evil people. To my face at least. In part, this was due to my award-winning acting. I had practice with her Aunt and Uncle at their store. Luckily, neither of them could make it. Otherwise, I might have convinced myself to work for them. Throughout the weekend, I never broke character. I even went to church with them. Of all things. The pastor's sermon was a wild nonsensical hodgepodge of bizarre thoughts that paraded under the banner of traditional normalcy. It was jazz without music. He praised our President for leading us down a righteous path. Recently our President had been in the news for election fraud and for attacking our basic civil rights. The pastor went on to praise god for blessing himself with such a beautiful and talented family. He told us god was good. This always struck me as an odd assumption. I think the best what we can hope for, if god exists, is that god is indifferent. But much more likely, as the evidence will show, god is probably downright evil. This is not a judgement being passed on god, it is more of an objective observation of previous behaviors. However. Everything will be revealed in the end. Or not. Regardless. When I reflect on anything that brought me genuine meaning and pleasure in this lifetime, it never revolved around a high stakes guessing game (in theory), and it was never something that worked to problematically divide me against others (in practice). However. For the sake of the mystery surrounding an all-powerful higher-Being, individuals with far greater talents could provide a more compelling illusion than this hack at the pulpit. Still. The illusion was not enough. I needed a better illusion.

Modern living occurs via incremental stages. You can only succeed to the next stage if you are able to lie to yourself about the following: I have not become an incredibly boring person who does incredibly boring things; I have not become submissive, unimaginative, and no fun at all; I still stand for everything I previously stood for; I am doing what I originally planned on doing; and this new me prefers to pour over minute details for minimal pay while putting up with shit from people who are not as talented as I am. If you believe these lies, you will be successful. You will move up to the higher levels they have planned out for you. The more submissive, the more successful. The more power you place over yourself, the more successful you will be. The deeper you bury yourself into submission, the more successful you will be.

If you were trapped in mental isolation for five hundred years, how many times would you lose your mind? How many times would you find it again? At one point would you be able to go back and perfectly recite everything that happened when you were living?

The worst people are those who write books. Books proclaiming to have insight into a right way of life. A better way to live. This is the worst type of person. A liar of the highest degree. They have only led people astray. Since time immemorial. They are the ones who created gods. Science. Everything in-between.

I was sitting on the couch. All of a sudden, I was waiting for the bus. I don't know what happened in between those two points in time. I remember what I was thinking. I thought of another possibility. We were created by some higher-Being or gods as a highly automated system. We can worship these higher-Beings all we want. However. They might never check in on us. We create satellites and release them into the heavens. They do work for us. Eventually they are left to wander the universe. Flung out into space to drift forever unmonitored. We are the same. A trinket. A gadget. One of their student's science fair projects. Everything we do is highly predictable. It always has been. Humanity has always centered around very basic functions. It always will. Oh well.

It's never the right people who commit suicide. It's always the people who everyone hates to see go. They were going through a difficult time. They had problems they couldn't work out. No genuinely evil person has a moment of deep insight: "I really shouldn't be doing any of this. I am a truly horrible person. I need to kill myself to prevent myself from physically harming these people." But this never happens. There are ruthless dictators and suicide bombers who commit suicide before they are captured, but their timing is off.

I was struck by a thought on my way to the store. Maybe it's the opposite of what I've always thought? I put everyone around me in the most difficult situations. All the time. With every move I make. It's not me that has it the worst. It's everyone else. They are the ones made to suffer the greatest moral dilemmas and anxieties because of my actions. How would I be able to tell? Could I do anything? My only options to prevent harming others would be to do nothing from here on out, or go insane attempting to predict how each action is going to negatively effect everyone. So I'm back to being in the worst position. This is why the opposite is never the opposite. I bought assorted fruits and vegetables.

I was still on the airplane. A baby cried the entire flight. When we are babies, parents take dangerous objects away from us. Toys we are not old enough to play with. We do not yet know how to use them. They replace the dangerous objects with something safer in order to pacify us. Sometimes we notice and put up a fuss. Eventually we have to move on. Other times we don't even notice. What force plays the paternal role for adults? The government? The law? The police? The economy? The perceived economy of time? It directs and regulates. It makes me choose a job I don't want but feel obligated to take. In so many instances, why do I feel as if there is no other way? I need to do it for the parent. For society. Complete happenstance. I need to fill the role I've been placed into. I give up the roles utilizing my talents. I give up on dreams. In all aspects of my life, I settle for less. In order to pacify. It is safer this way. Do I feel the policing paternal force acting upon me? Or have our parents abandoned us?

I had a dream I was an aspiring young filmmaker. I was premiering one of my films at a film festival. The screening went very well. The Q and A went very well. The night was light and breezy. The drinks were stiff. The city was old. The girls were young. After the screening, I introduced myself to an individual who had been roaming around the same circle of people. He told me my approach was all wrong. That I shouldn't simply introduce myself. He asked me if I knew who he was. He told me that he was the person that could have funded my next film...if I had gone about introducing myself the right way. Clearly, he thought he was very important. He asked me what my next project was. I didn't understand why we were still talking. I told him. Then he tore it apart. He asked me what my favorite film was. Then he tore it apart. He said it was obvious. I told him I chose it because I was sure he wouldn't be familiar with my actual favorite film. Which I told him. For a couple seconds he pretended. Then I quizzed him on who the director was. Now he was on his heels. I told him, "You might have a lot of money, but you don't know shit about film." He told me that he was starting to like me. I told him to fuck off. Then I woke up, regretting my inability to network. I couldn't be too upset. I had gotten much farther than I ever had in real life.

In the simulation of life, they will always have something to be able to pin on you at any given moment. You can always be in the wrong at any given moment. Most of the time. In very drastic ways. You have to be perfect. You will go insane attempting perfection. Or attempting perfection is the only way out of this mess. It's impossible to know. Oh well. However. Unfortunately. Veering wildly from the path of perfection is at times the only way to achieve it. There is no way to win. Winning is hardly the point. Oh well. Never give them an opportunity to exploit you. They will. If it pleases them to do so. It does please them to do so. Especially when everything is going wrong. It will always only get worse. It's not just that everything that can go wrong will go wrong; it's also the case that everything will go wrong ever-so-slightly so that you can't tell if everything is constantly going wrong all the time or if it's just your imagination, and you won't know how it is going wrong, and you won't have anything else to compare it to.

I remember one of my superiors from the past. He was a perfectly incapable man. He rose to the top because he never went away. The other idiots at the top had no idea. He could talk his way into and out of anything—with them. Talking to this specific brand of idiot was all he could do. Moving was difficult. He was morbidly obese. This did not prevent him from hitting on me. Those attempting to accomplish something always wished he'd leave as soon as he arrived. He was a visionless visionary. He thought highly of his business acumen. He would use the same sales pitch for caskets, as he would for ice cream. He lacked all tact and strategic planning. He lacked the ability to take money from corporate backers, nod his head "Yes" when they told him their vision, and then turn to his team, and say, "Okay, that's great, but we are going to make something better than what they think they want." Instead he merely followed the visionless idiots. They didn't know what they wanted. He didn't know what he wanted. It was up to us to make something out of the crap handed to us. Correction. It was up to me to make something out of the crap handed to us. He thought of himself as an artist. He wasn't. He always said, "Great artists steal" (he spoke in clichés often, or, rather, when he spoke, he instantly turned whatever he was saying into a cliché). Apparently this gave him license to literally take ideas from others. He didn't tweak them. He didn't add anything to them. He just stole them.

I was watching a nature documentary. It was a weekday. Or a weekend.

A particular insect was made to pollenate so many hundreds of plants a day in order to get their nutrients. Over deep time, the plants had learned to train the insect for their benefit. Did the insect know the system was rigged? Were they merely playing along with the plant's game and knew there was no other way? Or were they totally oblivious? If they did know, could they radically circumvent millions of years of evolution and gain the upper hand? Could they bypass/hack/decode the underlying universal language that contains the logic and creative possibilities? Or are there evolutionary biological/psychological safeguards that prevent them from knowing the game is rigged without them simultaneously knowing how to design a better system than the rigged one they are subjected to? Wouldn't it be a devastating event for their civilization, for their way of life, and for their psyche to fully understand their plight? However, if some members of their civilization knew their plight (perhaps they wrote about it in books), and other members of their civilization (perhaps organized into powerful institutions) knew how to design a better system. The question remains: why didn't they do anything to change it?

I was standing in line at the bank. No I wasn't. I was sitting at work. This must have been many years ago. A thought struck me about the projects I worked on over the years. Part of us, or all of us, can get trapped into one or all of our projects when we die. Or maybe we are allowed to escape. Just in case... Whatever we create, we should place an eternal paradise somewhere in the project. I look back. My earlier projects. I did not do this. Had I stopped there, I would have doomed myself to an eternal hell of cheesy, underdeveloped, jejune, themes revolving around bitterly adolescent romantic ideals. Perhaps this is why so many great artists ask their loved one's to destroy their work when they are on their deathbed. They don't want to haunt their works for eternity. They want to be able to dissolve completely. To be reborn as something else completely.

Curiosity is never wrong. I realized this when watching a small child playing. I was trapped. Again. At another family gathering. Indoors. In the suburbs. I was sitting with my compatriots in brilliant silence. One of our own wandered off from the pack. The toddler was playing with a variety of toys set out for him in the "living" room. Due to the homeowner's blatant disregard for humanity's aesthetic achievements, the room should have been named: the "clinging to life" room. The toddler stopped. Abruptly. I watched the toddler. Waiting for him to provide an answer. He ran over to the window. All serious and excited. He pointed at the loud machinery outside. Absent mindedly, without looking up, I said, "Yes, garbage truck." After a few seconds I realized my blunder. It was too late in the day for a garbage truck. I went over to the window. I saw a large dump truck full of dirt pulling up to the neighbor's house. I was completely wrong. The small child's curiosity was not. My judgments came and went. His curiosity remained.

I left my shoddy apartment to go to the diner. I ended up at the laundromat. I had brought my clothes. So I decided to wash them. All the while, I thought to myself. Something is preventing me from finding out. I'm stabbing in the dark. Too slow. The meaning of everything. Glances by me. The higher-power dodges behind a corner. My eyes glimpse a shadow. Suspicion and paranoia. I never know. Unless my eyes catch up. They find myself. I am the mastermind who prevents and holds me back. We'll see. Or not. What am I supposed to find? What is preventing me from finding it? It can't be the government. Too simplistic. Too obvious. Not in their best interests. Too much elaborate planning. Right? Or is that what they want me to think? The higher-Beings? The lower-beings? Too far fetched. Or is that what they want me to think? Does the higher-power that prevents me from finding out even know it's preventing me from finding out? Back to myself as the mastermind. Why am I preventing myself from knowing everything? From getting what I want. From living my life. What helps create this willing/self-imposed forgetfulness: the illusion that we aren't in complete control of everything. If we realize we control everything, and we create reality from scratch every second, the individual will become paralyzed with terror: how could we possibly generate our reality second by second, from whole cloth, and all by ourselves? All alone? Nobody else? In all of existence? And if we are doing all this ourselves why are we so bad at it? Why don't we give ourselves everything we want? Or at least most of what we want? Because we have to hide it from ourselves. We need incredible illusions to distract, either from our terrifying reality (higher-lifeforms must have already mastered the fear of being in complete control of their existence) or from what is a very dangerous delusion that has simply been lying in wait, at a particular stage in all human-esque civilizations as a test to see if the human-esque civilization can make it to the next level or be wiped out completely by this "thought disease." There have been several other smaller "thought diseases" humanity has withstood: unreasonable fears about gods, the night, monsters, witches, apocalyptic narratives, etc. So if everything all of a sudden starts happening exactly the way you want it to happen (as seen in various movies), that either means this theory is correct, and maybe you are ready to abandon the illusion that you aren't in control of everything, or it means that your reality is not real and you might be suspended in a dream state of some sort. Either way, I say go for it. Live it up all you can. But if none of this is correct, then you must ask what is my/the higher-power's end game? In all of these scenarios I can't imagine what anyone could gain from pulling the wool this far over my eyes. What am I providing for them? What are they gaining? What are they keeping me from? What are they preventing me from doing? But these are the wrong questions. But that is what they would want me to think. Oh well. Or I am over thinking it. The petty rivalries (that I fail to engage in) fueled by other people's shadowy jealousy have been holding me back. They go out of their way to make sure I do not succeed. Exactly what I think has happened has happened. I'm simply not participating in life. Too busy assuming my purpose is greater. It is not.

Unable to find a steady job and unable to pay rent, I accepted the offer extended by my lover who was not my lover. I moved into her apartment. My hand was forced. Not yet two weeks into the arrangement she sprung it on me, "I love you." She had me. The house always wins. Having been in this situation before, I knew this was not a standalone expression of affection. This was a heavily loaded question aimed directly at me. There was no hiding. There was only one correct answer. There was no time for hesitation in providing this one correct answer: "I love you too." And I meant it. In the sense that I loved her, as I loved all humanity. In the sense that I loved her for being a kind and generous human being who enjoyed the time we spent together. I am certain she meant it differently. She was in a celebratory mood. My gut was in my feet for weeks. We went out to a movie that night. During the movie there was a funny coincidence—the kind that only occurs in bad fiction. The characters on the screen acted out a scene very similar to our earlier exchange. However. In the movie, the result was a humorous disaster. My lover who now definitely thought she was my lover leaned over to whisper, "Good thing you didn't respond like that! But you wouldn't, of course, because we have something real!" I just smiled and nodded. I had a feeling I would be doing a lot of smiling and nodding. I had been doing it my entire life. There was no reason to stop now. I was finally good at something.

Language developed (and therefore meaning/logic) out of a primordial scream (eventually refined through frequent repetition) that was attempting (out of pure existential desperation and terror) to release the screamer from the downwarding spiral of an eternal dark nothingness. The scream was not in opposition to insanity. It was merely another form of it. The scream was insanity played out in a tangibly communal form. It was gripping. It provided a grounding, a momentary stability from which other things could follow. It was a marker that could differentiate. It could break the infinite darkness. Distinguish one's self from others. Etc. It created the madness of narrative. Individuals don't go mad, it's all madness, but the mad individual simply wanders too far outside the inner-circle of normative madness. Where the illusion has the strongest pull. Consciousness is always pure madness; it's a social contract of madness bound together by the madness of language. Rebuilding your mind from trauma, a baby's anxiety in realizing it is alive, the prehistoric humans developing the mind/language/culture, fixing the central problems at the heart of society, these are all one. All based on the terrible knowledge of existence, the knowledge of our death, without knowing what happens when we die. The knowledge of how ill-equipped we are to face that non-existence without meaning, without language, without consciousness. The collective unconscious returns. It haunts us. Unsolvable problems. Perhaps. Never to be solved. Therefore, these ghosts haunt us. The mistakes we make. Part of our routine to avoid the unsolvable. We make these mistakes as individuals, as societies, as a world. How do we equip ourselves to face them? And when we can't, what gets us out of the anxiety attack? Enough to get by. To live another day. Move further from the unanswerable. What gets us out of the infinity loop of multiplicity? Language? Helping others? A helping language. Through others. Is it merely in the doing? An action. A task to distract. Animal instinct. Everything springs out of this. All motivation. To get out of the anxiety/infinity loop of nothingness. Less developed forms of consciousness might remain stuck within it. Or they are free. And we are stuck. That instant. Having to build your reality from scratch. We do it every instant. We don't see it. Slow it down to a still-frame. We have entered the infinity loop. Like a needle skipping on a record player. We get out of it through language. Through meaning. We are able to speed the projector up again. We are able to get out of the still-fame and onto the next frame of the film. Yes, it is a lie. Yes, it is an illusion. But it makes everything exist. Paradoxes and jokes remind us it is a lie. They do so without us experiencing the instantaneous over-bearing force brought down upon us. The force of truth can fix people in the anxiety/infinity loop of multiplicity where everything breaks down. They aren't wrong. Everything breaks down. They are seeing the reality illusion for what it is. They need to be welcomed back into the illusion of language and meaning. Of doing and actions. Of helping others through language. This might not be possible. But their thinking isn't faulty. They are merely truly experiencing existence as it is: a painful anxiety ridden experience of being stuck in the multiplicity of all simultaneous meaning and noth-ingness, forced to generate all reality each moment with no shorthand to work with. Every second they have to create their reality from scratch. They have to create reasons why everything is the way it is. They are continually doubting, redoubting, and justifying why. Spending all of their time and energy on this endeavor while others simply believe. The person who is able to do this is an extraordinary genius. They will have nothing to show for it. And perhaps you are the only one doing it for everyone. After all, you are the only one you know who is thinking. You are the only one who you can be truly certain who is actually experiencing reality. Perhaps reality is being created through you for everyone. You are the one, quite literally, who is projecting reality for everyone, not just for you. But this thinking can get you stuck in the still-frame. I wonder why I haven't been stuck within this form of madness. Or maybe I have. I wonder if I would be able to tell. Oh well.

I wandered from window to window. I guess it never really mattered. In the past I was waiting in line to make copies at work. I was waiting in line at the bank. I guess it never really mattered. I found myself here. I found myself there. I guess it never really mattered. I was considering how to teach an entire skill or subject instantly. The student need not spend years practicing. To accomplish this the teacher should not dwell on how to teach the subject itself, but the worthiness of the subject being taught. The student won't be able to learn it instantly if there is nothing there worth learning. It's impossible to learn something instantly because it's impossible to learn anything at all. If you could learn anything, you could learn it instantly. The nature of learning is forgetting and remembering. It is perpetual stumbling. The same problem presents itself in time travel. The moment itself isn't stable, so how could you travel to and from it? Time is relative. So when we consider time, we do so from a particular person's perspective within their own unstable dimension. So whose unstable dimension of time are you leaving and returning from? How do you leave an event that neither begins nor ends? How do you push against nothing? And how can you do this when the individual doesn't understand the very moment in time they themselves have perceived?

I became a bartender. For too many years. Now I am older than I should be. I look younger than I should look. The worst of all worlds when attempting to start a career. Or become a teenage heartthrob. Or do anything. In the real world.

There will come a time when people with great ideas won't have to be driven to crisis. To depression by others to achieve their vision. It is not as many believe. You do not have to be depressed or mentally ill to achieve your vision. The world is crazy. In order to make it through, you have to match the world's intensity just to achieve your vision. Somewhere inside, find a place to remain the same.

I was back at the grocery store. Or the laundromat. No I was at the grocery store. My thoughts were wandering toward the store mascot when a middle-aged couple approached me. "Hello! How have you been!" They said expectingly. They moved in too quickly and confidently for a sales pitch. They didn't look the type. But I proceeded with the conversation under the assumption it was a sales pitch. From perfect strangers. "Hey. Good." I hadn't been good. I didn't have the time nor the energy to explain how I had been. The intensity of their shinny bright faces staring intently at me instantly drained any energy I had mustered for the day.

It looked as if they wanted to hug me. "It's been so long!" This was not a sales pitch. These people knew me. Or they thought they knew me. Maybe they knew my doppelgänger. Or maybe I had crossed into another dimension by accident, and the other me in this dimension knew these people. Or this middle-aged couple was pulling a prank on me. Or I had been wasted when I met them. I talk to everyone when I'm drunk. But I couldn't see us in the same bar. Regardless. I was in too deep. "Yes, yes it has." Maybe if I kept playing along I would remember how I knew them. Or the conversation would naturally reveal how we knew each other. I was wrong. Nothing came back to me. They were so vacantly polite it was impossible to gain any useful information from the conversation. Or they were masterful government agent spies who were employing radical mind-defying interrogation techniques. I realized this halfway through the conversation. I made my answers more vague from that point on. At first I just went with it. I responded as if I was talking to a distant relative or the relatives of my lover who definitely thought she was my lover: the updates about my life were partly true and partly based off of plans I hadn't yet followed through on in order to make myself look much better than I actually was. The couple didn't appear too shocked by my life updates. So I was either the same person they thought I was, or the new life course I had plotted for the person I wasn't didn't veer off in a way that was too unbelievable. Or they were being polite. They were very polite. We parted with the hug they wanted to give when they first saw me. I felt a very deep connection to these people. I still had no idea who they were. They really liked me. Or they were just being polite. I would see them around town a handful of times after that. Every interaction was the same. To this day, it was one of my fondest friendships.

The unfounded ephemeral intuition. All shadows. Never providing a definitive answer. Never revealing the actors behind the masks. Sometimes I guess right. Sometimes I guess wrong. Or do I? What was my original guess? When did I guess it? So eager to predict the future. I am unable to rule out the possibility that I've made it all up. During my darkest hours. The most troubling stretches of my life. When the wheels fell off. They are left turning in place. Intuition should be blamed. Intuition should be thanked. It moves me deeper into the darkness of my universal conspiracy theory. It makes me act randomly. It pulls me out again. It allows it to contradict itself. The insane decision was the only sane thing to do. It prevented me from going insane. I made all the wrong decisions for what happened to be the right reason. Whereas when I was sane, I was making all the right decisions that produced the wrong result. For no reason. As you can see, these forces are not opposites at all. They merely provide the right push at the right time. The reasons are unclear. At best. I don't know who is running this show.

"Philosophy without philosophers. Science without method. Religion without gods. Language without meaning." This wouldn't make the catchiest bumper sticker.

How to create the illusion. How to find yourself within the illusion that your trajectory is the one you want. The one you have planned for. The one you had a hand in making. The great trick of cause and effect. Have we already instinctively found the right trajectory? My will to live was much stronger than my suspicions. I had to decide. I had been in the right trajectory all along. I told myself. Deciding to take institutionalized medication needed to be part of that trajectory now. I was more than apprehensive. I felt as if I had given up. As if I had lost. They had won. Was this ever my decision? What if other trajectories were forever closed to me? What if I lost part of myself? Soon I didn't care. This was about survival. Use anything you can to survive. I would answer those questions later. Survive. For now. It was trial and error. They don't always get it right at first. It wasn't pleasant. Especially if you run out of money. At times the cure was worse than the disease. It got better. I lost some things. I gained some things. I promised to always remain me. Survive. For now.

Being able to swing from extreme to extreme. To dream up the most spectacular illusion. This is not an illness. It is a gift. The world does not know how to use it yet.

Identity prevents virtuosity. Being overly self-reflexive causes you to trip over yourself. At times. The other extreme: traditional modes of being. These always promise freedom from self-reflexivity. Their identity has been hidden in time. But their freedom is fleeting. The drive towards perfection. A hard working, limiting, non-narcissistic way of being. Strict discipline in every aspect of life. Adhering to rules no matter how outdated. No matter how out of touch. Maybe they aren't wrong. Completely. Mostly. They are. Maybe not in their general thrust. When I consider my adolescence, the derailment of my focus on fundamental skills came from concerns of identity, popularity, chasing girls, etc. This path led to a lot of pointless introspection and debilitating self-doubt. More time was spent trying to find my own way, as opposed to honing skills (perhaps I over-exaggerate). Being skillful would have solved all my problems (perhaps I over-exaggerate). Instead I wander a path continually questioning my confidence. I'm barely kept alive. I wouldn't recommend it.

When there is no way to know. This is the pressure point. This is where you will find the loose ends. They unravel everything. If there is no way to know, there is no way to know. It defeats itself. This is how you get outside.

I was drunk. And stoned. My lover who definitely thought she was my lover had already gone to bed. She was protesting my intoxication by watching Television alone in her room. She didn't like it when I had fun. As I fell asleep on the couch. I saw the following on a newscast. In my dreams. The competition to be one of the most influential Beings on our planet is actually a matter of one's eternal survival. It turns out, the only way more advanced alien lifeforms will appreciate Earth Beings and ask the individuals to join them for eternity is to have the individual's ideas, self, voice, etc. broadcast via radio waves bouncing across the universe. These radio waves will allow the aliens to track down our planet, find the individual or bring them back to life (their technology is that advanced), give them eternal life, and invite the individual to live with them. These aliens have been monitoring the radio waves of various lifeforms, hoping for signs of intelligent life in the universe. They have been sorely disappointed.

Memories of autumn came back so suddenly. So complete and full. And her, for the first time. Flannel and jeans. Memories suppressed for so long. Golden. With a breeze. Bright days of possibility. I loved her smile.

One needs to be free to think the most outlandish thoughts without feeling the need to commit to any of them. This had been lost on my superiors. I remember struggling to stay awake during their presentations. I struggled to care. I struggled to remember if I was there at all. I always thought it was strange how other people thought it was strange how the greatest "serious" intellectuals who made fantastic contributions to human thought could have also spent their time with silly outlandish occult ideas that were of absolutely no use to anyone. These brilliant thinkers simply thought a lot of thoughts. Many of them were good. Many of them were bad. Many forces work to highlight the good and useful ideas: their society in the past, our present society, and these individuals themselves. And we all collectively work to suppress their bad ideas. However. The ideas that were "good" are still very outlandish. These brilliant individuals just happened to also have good arguments to back them up. Most of life prevents us from thinking outlandish thoughts. However, only the most outlandish thoughts make it. They make dramatic positive change. Most of life prevents us from believing that generating outlandish ideas is worthwhile. Life wants us to think that normalcy is beneficial. It never is. Or the outcome is the same either way. Think zany thoughts and you will be poor. Think normal thoughts and you will also be poor. Whether you think normal thoughts or zany thoughts you will be poor either way. Have depression and you will be creative. Have depression and you will not be creative. Whether you are creative or not, you will be depressed either way. Live a normal life and you will die. Live an outlandish life and you will also die. Whether you live a normal life or an outlandish life you will die either way.

There will never be an end to the pointless tasks I am subjected to throughout the day.

My mind wanders back. No matter where I am. To that first strange failure. My body rejected success outright. It wasn't the last. It never started anything. There was never anything to begin with. Only the perpetuation of that same strange failure. It was implemented by an entity above and outside my plane of existence. An invisible hand. I was a fish. They. The police officer pointing and laughing. Tapping on the uselessly bulletproof glass of my mobile-fish tank. Should have seen this coming. I didn't even have that much to drink. Nothing but a stupid misunderstanding. Just enough to prevent a joyous celebration. Just enough to prevent my life from being filled with meaning. With punctuation. Unfortunately, it was never anything more than another stupid misunderstanding. Should it have been severe and dramatic, I may have been released from my purgatory. I may have outrun the constant nip of lesser dogs at my heals.

Our President who was not my President interrupted our regularly scheduled programing to make an announcement. These interruptions occurred more frequently. Advertisements occurred more frequently. The uneducated viewer (they were increasing in number) assumed it was one continuous show. They weren't completely wrong. My non-President struck a somber, apologetic tone. I thought, "Oh no. What have you done?" In a foreign land, our military was supposed to be protecting civilians from the enemy. Our military accidentally bombed a wedding. Innocent people were killed instantly. For no reason. It was supposed to be a joyous occasion. My non-President's speech-writer attempted to off-set the tragedy with strategic phrases: "...the usual precision with which our military operates...," and "It reminds us what a gift life is. It reminds us how precious our families are." The images flashing across the screen during the following news report told a different story. The few mourning survivors. The faces of pure terror. Children. Blood soaked. Covered in debris. All of my problems. Paled. There was nothing I could do. All our initial reactions. It could have been me. Then. To explain it away. The reasons why it could never happen to me. Does knowledge of the event provide perspective? My mind is not evolved enough to process that knowledge. My lover who definitely thought she was my lover thought our President who was not my President's speech was "Pretty good," but she thought his tie was completely inappropriate for the occasion. Neither of us would ever help those children. If they ever existed.

Is it insane to slowly go insane or to admit that you might be slowly going insane when your sanity is the only currency allowing you to move in a society that basis everything on sanity?

Isn't it odd that we still haven't established an ability to account for or predict innovation? Why do we perpetually reject its practitioners? Are we collectively losing our sense of taste? Our collective sense of smell is being depleted. Luckily, our landfills will be overflowing soon.

Throughout history, a lot of important people have died from syphilis... so I decided to stop wearing protection when having sex with random strangers.

I was stuck in the past again. The useless rage supplied by my former superior. I couldn't get over the pure pointlessness of the visionless visionary's existence. He despised genuine talent. He insulated himself with clueless people whenever possible. Individuals with any vision or purpose threatened to expose him. Therefore, they must be disposed of. This was the only thing he was ever right about. After a couple months, I had a meeting scheduled with this megalomaniac. When I entered his office, he started the meeting by telling me I was fired. I was being fired because they simply ran out of money to keep me on the payroll. In the middle of the year. It was as simple as that. I was, of course, the only one doing any real work for the company. I didn't complain much. They were hurting themselves as much as they were hurting me. Luckily, everybody lost that day. Oh well.

Every suspicion. Creeping up on me. Something else is going on. Behind the scenes. There must be a conspiracy. There must be a higher-Being pulling the strings. There must be a fate we are blind to. There must be forces working against you. Or for you. All distractions. All wishful thinking to avoid the simple fact that you were born and you will die. Nothing will come from any of it. This is the only Truth. We move heaven and earth to distract ourselves from the disturbing fact: everything happens exactly as it appears to happen. Everything that happens to us is completely justified. Everything that happens to anyone is completely justified. All deaths are justified. All deaths are for nothing. There is nothing we can learn from anything.

There she was again. The female trapped with me in the Eternity Perfume advertisement. I was at the laundromat. No, I was standing in line at the bank. She was still with her not-as-attractive, nerdy husband. Briefly, I should mention a funny coincidence—the kind that only occurs in bad fiction. After our date (many years ago), she actually went on to model in a perfume advertisement. The perfume was named Eternity. Here, before me now, stood her husband and several smaller people. It took me some time to realize these must be children. Somehow they must have been created by the two adults who stood before me. But I concluded, more likely, science played a dominant role in their creation. We exchanged somewhat restrained pleasantries. Sparks were extinguished from her eyes. Where there was life was now lifeless. Every movement a trance. A black veil over every emotion. For the first time it struck me. I might be responsible for this. There now existed the possibility: I could be held accountable. Eternally. I had not been able to circumvent my own reactionary, judgmental, and insecure attitudes. I had not been able to usurp common order, norms, conveniences, rules, and laws to make the world do my bidding. It was my responsibility to bend the world to my will. Nobody else was going to. It was my responsibility to have taken her away from him. That would have been the right thing to do. It would have been destructive. It would have been chaotic. But it would have been justified. She would still be alive now. Maybe she wouldn't be with me. But she would still be her. She was no longer her. They talked about how happy they were with their careers and their children. I think he actually meant it. She did not. It was painfully obvious. As they parted, the family turned to leave. I started to say to her, "Maybe we should all…" Before I could finish she shook her head and walked away.

Yesterday or the day before I was starring out the window. Suddenly a low, rumbling background noise stopped. I hadn't been aware of it. It had been going on for hours. Maybe weeks. Maybe longer. I wonder if the end of my life was going to feel like this.

Do moments have lives?

Every individual needs projects to entertain the various people they are. We get anxious, stressed, and claustrophobic when we have no way to fully pursue a part of who we are. Our hero self need fans to cheer them on. Even if they are imaginary or few in number. Our poet self needs a life of silence to surround them. Even if it is an afternoon. Our rock star self needs a tumultuous gypsy life of constant change. Even if it is a roadtrip, a friendship, or open-mic night. Our comedic self needs people to laugh. Our intellectual self needs validation that we are smart, etc. When this doesn't happen, there is a direct, immediate, and predictable effect that takes place on us.

When we were younger, my buddies and I thought music was becoming too mainstream. We listened to plates being scratched by forks.

I am the least successful version of myself. I am the self who is left out of dreams. Dreams that my other selves in other realities are left to enjoy. I am the one who remains. I am the one who stays behind. The others move forward. Away from this purgatory. I am left behind with nothing to be proud of. When I start to get excited about something. When I start to feel alive. Rejection. Has your hard work ever paid off? Do you ever find satisfaction? Why do others find success and you don't? Isn't it strange that nothing is going your way? Especially the things that should definitely go your way? They never do. Everything is déjà vu. Everything has already happened to you. It keeps happening to you. It will continue to do so. My life is not my own. It is a tragically darkened comedy. It is played out for the entertainment of higher-lifeforms. They watch. They laugh. They cry. None of it is for me. Unless. I make it about me. How would I? Or I should make it less about me. How would I?

Sometimes I wonder what would happen if I wrote a book and injected a slew of pessimistic theoretical musings about the universe and pretended they were a joke. But then people started to take them seriously. Then humanity fell apart. I wonder how guilty I would feel. But nothing I plan ever comes to fruition. I have nothing to worry about.

A while ago, I met this man. He was a photographer for various travel magazines. He wanted to be a fine art photographer. Instead he traveled the world and took cheesy (to the trained eye) yet tasteful (to the untrained eye) travel photos. But he got to travel the world. He hated traveling. He told me he felt he was constantly standing outside his own story. Just barely. A step behind. He was never able to be a part of anything. People think of him as a certain person, but he is never able to fully embody this person. He fell in love with a woman. He married her sister. I never found out how this happened. He told me that when he dreams, everything is different. Everything is better. He is able to catch up to himself. He told me he thinks he has figured out that he has been trapped in a specific reality or different dimension because of some specific event in his life, but he can't figure out what it is. The rules of this dimension are all distractions to prevent him from realizing it. He is trying to figure out how to get to another dimension. In this new dimension he will be able to experience things more fully, like when he was a child, without the unpredictable and drastic emotional shifts of childhood. Correction, he used to be a photographer for various travel magazines. He was telling me all of this when we were at work. He used to work with me. A long time ago. I should mention that. I would have told our superiors about his mental state, but they probably would have taken him away. I would rather listen to his theories than listen to anything our superiors had to say. It made the boring day go by much faster. He was just as good at his job as anyone else. And probably more intelligent than our superiors. Most people were.

We get in trouble. We are penalized. For being people we never wanted to be. For taking positions we never wanted to take. For being in situations we never wanted to be in. We aren't given the ability to live the plan we wanted. Then we are penalized for living the plan someone else laid out for us. We are to blame for the decisions we make. We are to blame for the decisions that are made for us. Either way we lose.

They were very lazy when they named the orange.

And although this life might be a pointless game, a meaningless simulation, or all of you might be playing a trick on me, I might as well raise as much hell as possible while I'm here. Maybe I'm only imagining I'm raising hell. Maybe this is an empty gesture. Playing into the game even more. Oh well. I might as well imagine I am getting my kicks. Sure. I'll see if I can cause a ruckus while I play the game. Even if it's imaginary. I went to the store, and I was still in high spirits. I thought about stealing something to act on my new found rebelliousness. I couldn't decide what to steal. I got bored. I shopped and paid for everything as I had always done.

Silence doesn't always mean disagreement. As when a speaker (soon to be listener) reveals something controversial or secret and doesn't receive an immediate response. As when human existence shouts into the void of space/time and hears nothing in return. Sometimes. The responder simply doesn't know how to respond. Sometimes. The responder is struggling to conjure the most appropriate response. Sometimes. It's the opposite of what the eager listener first negatively assumes. Sometimes. It's the responder's care that generates this silence. But usually, not. Most of the time. The silence means the listener is on the wrong track. Completely. Most of the time. The silence means the listener needs to totally reassess what we are doing. This should not come as a surprise. It's safe to say that 99.9% the time we are on the wrong track. Regardless. But I could be wrong. Oh well.

The great puzzle in life is to figure out which part of ourselves is supposed to match up with which period of our lives and state of emotional/mental development. We are contorted and twisted. We are misaligned from the moment in time in which this specific part of ourselves was supposed to have been aligned with the time period we were supposed to have lived and the emotional and mental state in which we were supposed to have lived. The mechanism that has twisted us? Modernity, or a glitch in the simulation, or a faulty application of cause and effect, or a faulty sense of time, language, etc. We are perpetually dissatisfied. Because another aspect of our Being is supposed to live during the space in which we are occupying. We have guessed the order wrong. Our alignment is off. Our whole self is comprised of movable cylindrical segments rotating around a smaller vertical inner cylinder. Each cylindrical segment has a correct position in relation to the cylindrical segments above and below it. Much like a slot machine, everything needs to line up perfectly. For you to be aligned correctly. To twist yourself into the right position. To be in your correct space/time. To be perfectly where you should be. Being with the right lover. If you always find yourself either pining for someone in the past or someone in the future, you are misaligned. If you are restless then you are in the misaligned. You would much rather trade places for all the times when you wanted to settle down but couldn't. What mechanism can we use for this re-alignment? Some combination of a mechanical time-traveling device, intense meditation, virtual reality simulation, hallucinogens, and quantum mechanics?

Our President who was not my President decided to do nothing about the ridiculous cost of college and the amount of debt young people (not from upper class families) take on to receive their education. Our society penalizes those who are attempting to improve themselves and their world. It also penalizes those who don't attempt to improve themselves and their world. No matter what you do, our society wants to penalize you. But if you go to war and come back alive (albeit possibly mentally or physically maimed) you can attend college for free. If the cost of college wasn't egregious and everyone wasn't already being shot in their own neighborhood, nobody would join the military.

The higher-lifeforms keep hoping I'll end my own life. Somehow this version of me won't do it. They don't think I'm going to keep being risky. The risky decision to plod through the insanity that surrounds me. The risky decision to wade through this vast sea of shit. The higher-powers keep expecting me to settle. They have grown weary. If I continue, they must continue to generate the reality I inhabit. I have been reaching the limits of the simulation. They want me to stop. I will overpower them soon. Or go insane. It's the same. Oh well. They are developing writer's block. They are struggling to find different plots for my life that will appear authentic. This is fairly difficult because they have built a complex world around me. Not the most complex world they've ever made, but complex none-the-less. Everything has to shift perfectly. Otherwise, I will fail to believe I am still operating within the boundaries of this reality. Even when I'm believing that I'm not believing that I'm believing that I'm not believing, etc. For example, when I "fail" at a certain career, this event must be accompanied by an entire set of complex explanations. These explanations must appear organic. They must travel all the way out to my entire socio-political belief system. My upbringing. My sexuality. Etc. Not merely because the career never existed, but when any shift occurs it effects the entire landscape. It effects one's perception of space and time. Wait, why did they think I wouldn't last this long?

I thoroughly enjoy meeting people who travel the same speed as I do.

We should not follow proven ways. We should follow ways that are completely unprovable. We should follow ways that point to the silent failing of the machinery. These failings point to questions that need to be asked. Questions with no answers to present themselves. Questions that could garner no support from any community of learned scholars or from the public. This is where potential exists. This is also where you will ruin yourself. Oh well.

My lover who definitely thought she was my lover did not want me to be successful. She was the most unsupportive person I ever met. Or I wasn't talented. At anything. When we discussed future careers or the steps I should take to pull myself out of poverty, she attempted to dissuade me, lower my expectations, or poke holes in my plans. She was either devastatingly unhelpful or she was providing sound advice. But if her motivation was to keep me grounded, it was not ill-advised. If I did become successful, if I did go out into the world, I would probably leave her for the thousands of other females who would make a better match. It made perfect sense why she did not want me to be successful. Shouldn't I be worried about the thousands of other males she would make a better match with? Perhaps if I did this, I would be able to fall in love with her. I made plans to sabotage her career.

I stood at the bus stop. In line at the bank. Waiting for my laundry. Looking out the window of my apartment. What is the real reason I kept going? Not the pretty reasons I perpetually attempted to mold into theories. Was it my delusional thinking balanced by my practical output? My inability to believe in anything, including myself? My intense moments of belief followed by my intense and immediate rejection of that belief after it runs its course? Spending my time day dreaming every imaginable scenario and not staying on task? Being unpredictable (even to myself) thereby throwing the higher-powers off my scent? Being able to tell when I'm being duped? Not being able to tell when I'm being duped, but thinking that I'm being duped even when I'm not and therefore, by chance, I avoid being duped?

I found myself in the children's section of a bookstore. I'm not sure how this happened. Nostalgia took the wheel. It was running wild. The older books provided a smile of recognition. I opened newer books. They were shit. Except the ending of a particular book: "Even if everything is an illusion. Even if I'm sent into a million pieces by space and time. Flying across the vast expanses of space and eternity to wander forever. Even if our molecules should never reform as they are now. In this moment. I love you, my son."

When I was younger I considered becoming a famous author. When I was younger I never considered doing anything without becoming famous at it first. If I were an author now, I would write a story with a character who had no name. Trapped in pages and time. I hope this is not me. It might be. This character's purpose is perpetually uncertain. Their existence, more so. They only feel the demands. Placed on themselves by themselves and others. They live from expectation to deadline. This provides their life meaning. Until their expiration date. The end. I never said I'd be a good author. I never became an author. Or famous.

I remember summer nights turning cool. Playing in the backyard. Freshly cut grass. Running. Happy people. Never wanting it to end.

READERS GUIDE

1. What time period does the narrator live in? What evidence is provided to reach this conclusion?

2. What impact does the book's general ambiguity towards time have on the reader? Why/Is it interesting?

3. What details—that we typically look for/expect in books (and life)—are missing from the narrator's accounts?

4. Does the lack of typical details (or narrative guide posts) affect the reader's experience? How so?

5. What is the narrator's age, gender, sexuality? What are you (the reader) basing these assumptions on? Why does it matter? How does it affect the story?

6. How long does it take you to adjust to this episodic/anecdotal form of storytelling? Or do you ever adjust?

7. How does the form of this book—brief episodic glimpses questionably connected to the whole—affect the content of this book?

8. Under the assumption that it can (or any book can) be placed within a specific genre, what genre does this book fall under? Humor?

Tragedy? Literary? Low-brow? Horror? Philosophy? Sci-fi?

9. Assuming that this book can be placed in any of the aforementioned genres, what changes (what is highlighted or brought out of the text) when the book is placed within one of these contexts? In other words, how would the reader experience this book differently if it was listed as humor, or horror, or philosophy?

10. What moments in the book did you feel emotional ambivalent or emotionally confused: you could not tell if something was funny or sad, intellectual or silly, etc.?

11. What is the point of writing a book that doesn't discern whether these musings are intellectually rigorous, the signs of mental illness, or an elaborate trick at our expense? Is this/Why is it difficult to discern what category each anecdote fits in? What does this say about our own "modern" condition? In other words, who has a skewed perception of reality: the narrator, his society, or ourselves?

12. How much do we trust the narrator's accounts to be an accurate representation of his world? What makes us trust/untrust the narrator's accounts (his love life, etc)?

13. What is preventing the narrator from making major life decisions? Does the narrator know what he wants? Is another part of him making these decisions? What part of him (multiple/other identity within himself) is making these decisions? His subconscious? What else?

www.ingramcontent.com/pod-product-compliance
Lightning Source LLC
Chambersburg PA
CBHW022010080426
42733CB00007B/556